Sylvia
I hope you are
encouraged by God's
word and remember

> **W**e <u>know</u> that all things
> work together for good
> to those who love God, to
> those who are the called
> according to His purpose.
>
> ROMANS 8:28 NKJV

... so don't forget — you
know what you know!!
XXOO
much love

THE 100
MOST IMPORTANT
BIBLE VERSES
FOR WOMEN

Presented to:

Beautiful,
Sylvia

Presented by: *Your friend forever*
and sister in Christ
Pam

Date:

December 18th 2006

I will meditate on Your precepts, and contemplate Your ways. I will delight myself in Your statutes; I will not forget Your word.

PSALM 119:15–16 NKJV

THE 100 MOST IMPORTANT BIBLE VERSES FOR WOMEN

W PUBLISHING GROUP
A Division of Thomas Nelson Publishers
Since 1798

www.wpublishinggroup.com

The 100 Most Important Bible Verses for Women
©2005 by GRQ, Inc.
Brentwood, Tennessee 37027

Published by W Publishing Group, a Division of Thomas Nelson, Inc., P.O. Box 141000, Nashville, Tennessee 37214.

W Publishing Group books may be purchased in bulk for educational, business, fundraising, or sales promotional use. For information, please email SpecialMarkets@ThomasNelson.com.

Scripture quotations are from the following sources:

• The New Century Version® (NCV). Copyright © 1987, 1988, 1991 by Word Publishing, a Division of Thomas Nelson, Inc. Used by permission. All rights reserved. • The New King James Version® (NKJV), copyright © 1979, 1980, 1982, Thomas Nelson, Inc., Publishers. • The Contemporary English Version (CEV) © 1991 by the American Bible Society. Used by permission. • The Holy Bible, New International Version (NIV). Copyright © 1973, 1978, 1984, International Bible Society. Used by permission of Zondervan Bible Publishers. • The Living Bible (TLB), copyright © 1971 by Tyndale House Publishers, Wheaton, Ill. Used by permission. • New American Standard Bible (NASB), © 1960, 1977, 1995 by the Lockman Foundation. • New Living Translation (NLT), copyright © 1996 by Tyndale House Publishers, Inc., Wheaton, Ill. All rights reserved. • The Message (MSG), copyright ©1993. Used by permission of NavPress Publishing Group.

Managing Editor: Lila Empson
Associate Editor: Laura Kendall
Manuscript: Jeanette and Mark Littleton
Design: Thatcher Design, Nashville, Tennessee

Library of Congress Cataloging-in-Publication Data
100 most important Bible verses for women.
   p. cm.
ISBN 0-8499-0029-8
1. Christian women — Religious life. 2. Bible — Qutotations. I. Title: One hundred most important Bible verses for women. II. W Publishing Group.

BV4527.A14 2005
220.5'2 — dc22

                                    2005010084

Printed in China.
05 06 07 08 — 9 8 7 6 5 4 3 2 1

If any of you needs wisdom, you should ask God for it. He is generous and enjoys giving to all people, so he will give you wisdom.

JAMES 1:5 NCV

Contents

Your promises are sweet to me, sweeter than honey in my mouth!

PSALM 119:103 NCV

Introduction

God loves you as part of his creation, and he also loves you individually for who you are. He loves your spirit and your soul. He loves the personality that makes you uniquely you.

You'll find more about the vastness of God's love for you as you look through the pages of the Bible. The Bible is God's love letter to you, and this love letter is filled with his promises.

Those promises especially apply to you. As a busy woman in today's world, you have specific needs, concerns, and activities in your life. God directly addresses those areas through the Bible. The Bible offers, hope, help, challenge, encouragement, and wisdom for every situation a woman can face today. If you have questions, the Bible can give you answers.

The 100 Most Important Bible Verses for Women is designed to help you find vital words of affirmation and advice from God. Each brief chapter highlights a bite-size portion of the Bible that addresses your spiritual, emotional, physical, and relational needs as a woman. Every page offers you insight that you can easily apply in your life.

Fall in love all over again—with God, and with his Word. Relish his promises and draw strength from his support and life-changing truth. Through *The 100 Most Important Bible Verses for Women*, discover what he's saying to you, from his heart to yours.

Be still, and know that I am God; I will be exalted among the nations, I will be exalted in the earth!

PSALM 46:10 NKJV

Quiet amid Chaos

Three words can aptly describe the average woman today: *busy, busy, busy.* She hurries from one project or need to another, taking care of others and balancing demands. Studies show that not only is the average woman busy from the time she gets up to the time she goes to bed, but she also is reducing her sleep time because she has too much to do.

It is tough for many women to slow down for anything—even God. This not only affects a woman's physical life, but also her spiritual life. It is important for women to be still and know God for a couple of reasons. In taking time to be with God, a woman builds her relationship with him. As she focuses on God, she remembers how vast God is. She thinks about

> **It is important for women to be still and know God for a couple of reasons.**

God knowing everything, being everywhere, and being the focus of the universe. That puts her life into perspective as she sees the big picture of God and takes the focus off her own limited world. Perhaps most important, when a woman is still, she is refreshed spiritually and gains a new sense of how important she is to God. As a woman is still before God, she hears his voice—his loving, supportive, reassuring voice.

Slow down. Avoid being so busy with the necessities of life that you forget to nourish your soul. Take time to be still in God's vastness. Somehow everything important will get done, and you'll find fresh rest for your life.

God loved the world so much that he gave his one and only Son so that whoever believes in him may not be lost, but have eternal life.

JOHN 3:16 NCV

What God Did Just for You

The famous verse John 3:16 is an important one for all women. It speaks of God's love for you and of his great gift to you: eternal life.

God loves you more than you can imagine. He loves the whole world. God's love is inextinguishable, eternal, personal, and life-giving. That love is yours for the taking. Just accept it at face value, and God will be pleased. God has given you more than anyone would ever expect. He might have given you money or a mansion or a handsome husband or any number of other things for your enjoyment. But what he gave—his Son—encompasses all those things. God gave everything for you.

God made it as simple as possible to come to know him. What does he ask of you? Faith. Simply believe in his Son. Believe that what God says is true. That's it. Nothing more is needed. There is very little in life that is simpler or easier than that. God has made it uncomplicated and always available; he wants everyone to accept his gift. Anyone willing to accept and believe in Jesus gains all of God's blessings. God gave the greatest gift possible: eternal life, and that includes everything else in life—love, joy, peace, a home in heaven, friends. He has held nothing back.

> **God's love is inextinguishable, eternal, personal, and life-giving.**

You obtain all these grand blessings by faith, as the verse says. It remains a great promise to women of all ages and places. Simply by believing in Jesus, you can gain the greatest blessings God has to offer.

"**I** say this because I know what I am planning for you," says the LORD. "I have good plans for you, not plans to hurt you. I will give you hope and a good future."

JEREMIAH 29:11 NCV

Showers of Hope and a Sunshiny Future

When it comes to surprise parties, it's sometimes hard to figure out who enjoys the party most—the person being honored or the person doing the planning. Scheming good things for other people can be a blast. God shares the enjoyment of planning good things for people who love him.

Some people interpret Jeremiah 29:11 to mean that when a person loves God, everything in her life will be perfect. That's not necessarily true. Yes, in this verse, God promised the Israelites a great future. But before all the wonderful things happened, God knew the Israelites would be enslaved by the Babylonians for seventy years. He also knew that at the end, he would return them to their homeland and build a new nation committed to him and to his work.

Many Israelites probably wondered if their servitude would ever end. They worried that they'd die forgotten and enslaved. God assured them that he had a plan for their lives. He would carry out that design day by day. In fact, this strategy was so wonderful

> **God shares the enjoyment of planning good things for people who love him.**

that every person who heard it could have hope and sense that the future would be different, better, and even beautiful.

In the Bible, God repeatedly shows care and a great love for his people. He knows each person and has mapped out a plan to grant that person ultimate joy in life and a sense of expectation about the future.

God has a plan for you, for your loved ones, for everyone who loves him. He may lead you through grim times occasionally, but he has a great future full of happiness for everyone who relies on him.

Have I not commanded you? Be strong and of good courage; do not be afraid, nor be dismayed, for the LORD your God is with you wherever you go.

JOSHUA 1:9 NKJV

The God Who Is with You

Joshua must have felt overwhelmed. Moses had died and left him in charge. Moses had led the Israelites out of slavery in Egypt, and Joshua was to lead them into the land they'd been seeking for forty years. Joshua commanded an unruly group of vagabond families, and one of the first tasks on the agenda called for them to fight their way into the land God had promised. Joshua probably thought he couldn't do it, but God gave him reassurance.

When you face seemingly endless household tasks or unruly children or a stress-filled schedule and no time, perhaps you relate to Joshua. You are expected to take hold of the promised land of living faithfully for God in an unfaithful world. You look at your schedule and the amount of work to be done, and you cry, "I can't do this."

God offers you the same reassurance he gave Joshua. You can be strong and courageous. You can be confident and worry-free. You can rest in the understanding that God will give you what you need. When you feel overwhelmed, know that God is with you every step of the way—every step as you work in your home, as you run errands, as you care for others. God walks with you and infuses you with strength, courage, and confidence.

> You can rest in the understanding that God will give you what you need.

When you don't have power, God will empower you. When you don't have the strength, let God step in and give you the strength. Let him work in you and through you. He's willing to—every step of the way.

Mary brought in a pint of very expensive perfume made from pure nard. She poured the perfume on Jesus' feet, and then she wiped his feet with her hair. And the sweet smell from the perfume filled the whole house.

JOHN 12:3 NCV

The Sweet Scent of Worship

Imagine that you're at a home Bible study. All of a sudden, a classy, if not wealthy, woman drops to her knees and washes the Bible study leader's feet with Clive Christian #1, one of the world's most expensive perfumes.

That act would stay in your memory and be a conversation topic for a long time. And that's the reaction people had when Mary anointed Jesus's feet. Actually, several shocking things occurred. The woman's expensive perfume was probably a treasure she'd hoarded. In a culture where women generally acted discreetly around men, she made a spectacle of herself. And in her culture, the foot was considered a rude, nearly unmentionable part of the body. But Mary not only poured her expensive perfume on Jesus's feet, she also used her hair—considered a woman's glory—to wipe his feet.

Why did Mary act in such an unorthodox manner? She wanted to give Jesus her best possession and the most honored part of herself. She wanted to worship him, even though it meant sacrifice.

Real power comes through worship. Through worship, you give God honor. And just as Mary's perfume was a sweet fragrance wafting in the air, your worship is a delectable fragrance to God. By her actions, Mary showed the truest and greatest gift any woman can offer God: worship. Mary's actions sprang from heart, and John 12:3 is a message of God's greatest desire and a woman's greatest gift to him in one stop.

> **Real power comes through worship. Through worship, you give God honor.**

Joyous and sacrificial worship comes in many forms. Whatever your gift, give it to God, and let the fragrance of worship refresh him and strengthen your heart.

We know that all things work together for good to those who love God, to those who are the called according to His purpose.

ROMANS 8:28 NKJV

All Things

Kim always felt the worst thing that could ever happen was for a person to lose his or her job. So when her boss told her that her position was being eliminated because of budget cuts, she was shocked. She had three months left to find another job, and the company had no openings at her management level. "Actually, losing my job was the best thing that ever happened to me," Kim says today. "It forced me to try to start my own business. And thanks to that, I can work from home and be there for my kids."

Whenever unfortunate events or even tragedies happen, you hear people murmur, "Well, they say everything happens for the best." Often these folks don't realize they're quoting a scriptural promise found in Romans 8:28. God is aware of every situation you encounter, and he can fit it all into the master plan for your life.

> **God is aware of every situation you encounter, and he can fit it all into the master plan for your life.**

That doesn't mean everything that happens to you will be good. You live in a world where problems and difficulties happen daily, where bad things strike without notice, to all people. But no matter what happens in your life, God promises he will use it—even the tragedies—for some redeeming purpose. He is Lord in your life, during the good days and even in the bad moments.

Today, no matter what life throws at you, rest in the promise and the hope that God can use anything, good or bad, to create the beautiful tapestry of your life.

Ruth said: "Entreat me not to leave you, or to turn back from following after you; for wherever you go, I will go; and wherever you lodge, I will lodge; your people shall be my people, and your God, my God."

RUTH 1:16 NKJV

Loyalty Is a Choice

One of life's most joyous elements is relationships. All people are relational, building intimacy and love with relatives, friends, and acquaintances. Undoubtedly, you have many important and close contacts in your life that you value and cherish. You want to build and sustain close relationships. You want to make them even more intimate, and more compelling.

This most important passage from the Bible shows Ruth relating to her mother-in-law, Naomi. With both of their lives devastated by death and disease, they ended up widows in a foreign land. When Naomi told Ruth to return to her people, Ruth resisted. Her loyalty to Naomi was so intense that she wanted to go with Naomi back to her homeland.

Ruth said she would stay with Naomi, live where she lived, accept Naomi's people as her own, and worship the same God Naomi worshiped.

> **Ruth said she would stay with Naomi, live where she lived, accept Naomi's people as her own, and worship the same God Naomi worshiped.**

What drove Ruth to this commitment? Scholars might answer many ways—love, a sense of moral right, a realization that without Naomi she had nothing—but one answer is paramount: Ruth chose to remain loyal to Naomi. She could have gone back to her people, no questions asked. But she chose to love, follow, and live with Naomi.

Ruth's decision to stay with Naomi demonstrates the essence of commitment to another person: it is a choice you make every day.

~

Take a look at the choices you make in your relationships. Work at being loyal, loving, giving, honest, forthright, and vulnerable. Loyalty will seal your relationships and make you one who is trusted and loved.

I will bless her, and indeed I will give you a son by her. Then I will bless her, and she shall be a mother of nations; kings of peoples will come from her.

GENESIS 17:16 NASB

God's Special Blessing

Most women sooner or later will seek some special blessing from God. They usually ask for something they really want. Instead of asking God for the blessing you desire, give God the opportunity to bless you the way he wants to. It is possible that God has a blessing for you that you could never imagine, but which, when granted, will make your life more beautiful and joyous than ever before.

At ninety years old, Sarah, Abraham's wife, had never had children. Probably in her earlier years, Sarah had prayed for a child. But as time wore her down and age wore her out, she probably gave up on hoping for that blessing. Even though when Abraham was seventy-five God had promised him a son (when Sarah was sixty-five), nothing happened for years. Finally, Sarah suggested that Abraham have a child with her maidservant, Hagar.

> Instead of asking God for the blessing you desire, give God the opportunity to bless you the way he wants to.

Sarah and Abraham were trying to fulfill God's promise through human means, and the culture in that day approved this method of producing an heir.

Ultimately, though, God rejected Hagar's son, Ishmael, and continued to promise Abraham that he'd have his own son through Sarah. The unexpected blessing came because Sarah wanted a child. God offered a son. Abraham wanted an heir. God made him the father of nations. God's personal blessing was far greater than the blessing Sarah sought.

—⁂—

Your blessing may not be a longed-for son. But if like Sarah you look to the Lord, his blessing will come. And it will bless you in the unique way only the God of grace can imagine.

Jesus answered, "If I want him to live until I come back, that is not your business. You follow me."

JOHN 21:22 NCV

"You Follow Me"

When Cheri learned that she was being laid off, she couldn't resist blurting out, "What about Pat?" Pat was at the same seniority level and position in the department. "Is Pat's position getting eliminated too?" "Let's just talk about you for right now, Cheri," her boss smoothly replied.

It is human nature for people to want to compare their plights to those of others. John 21:22 is no exception. Jesus had appeared to several of his disciples, including Peter—it was probably the first time the two had talked since he died and rose. In their conversation, Peter renewed his commitment to his leader. Then Jesus told Peter the big scoop—indicating how Peter would eventually die. You'd think

Peter might have a few questions or want to hear more details. Instead, Peter took a look around him and said, "So, what about John? Is he going to face the same kind of stuff I face?" That's when Jesus said, "Don't worry about him. You follow me."

People tend to get sidetracked by looking at others. Sometimes they want to make sure no one gets better treatment. They're so busy looking into other people's business with things like, "God, see the wrong stuff she did? What are you going to do about that, God?" When a person is watching and worrying about someone else's relationship with God, chances are that she's not taking the time to enjoy her own relationship with God. As with Peter and John, God tells you to follow the path he has created for you—no matter what happens to other people. You are not responsible for them; you are responsible for only yourself.

> When a person is watching and worrying about someone else's relationship with God, chances are that she's not taking the time to enjoy her own relationship with God.

Next time you're tempted to ask, "But what about . . ," bite your tongue and take the time to ask God how your relationship with him can improve.

Mary said, "I am the servant of the Lord. Let this happen to me as you say!" Then the angel went away.

LUKE 1:38 NCV

Mary, the Lord's Servant

Mary was probably only fourteen or fifteen years old when she learned that she was to become the mother of Jesus. She was years ahead of many women—and men, too—when it came to trusting God. Imagine how she must have felt. The man of her dreams had finally proposed. She was eagerly planning for the big wedding and happily-ever-after. Then God asked her to do something unbelievably difficult.

Mary was intelligent. As the angel explained the scenario, Mary immediately understood what this meant in light of the big picture. Pregnancy outside marriage meant she would be disgraced, possibly even stoned. Her family would suffer from that scorn; perhaps they would disbelieve her or turn on her. By placing her reputation in God's hands, Mary was risking the loss of the man she loved and the glorious future that was starting to unfold in her life. If she decided to trust God, her whole life might fall about her in ruins. But Mary was a woman of faith and trust. No negotiations. No whining. No pleading for a guarantee that her life would come out all right in the end. She just asked one technical question, "How can this impossible

> **Mary was a woman of faith and trust. No negotiations. No whining. No pleading for a guarantee that her life would come out all right in the end.**

thing happen?" And then she responded, "I am the Lord's servant. May it be unto me as you have said."

Mary's response to God as recorded in Luke 1:38 is an excellent model for women to emulate. God would like the same faithful and trusting response from you.

⊸⧽⊙

God may ask you to do things that will seem impossible. But as you trust and follow Mary's example, "May it be unto me," and you'll find that he walks with you through the impossible situations.

There is therefore now no condemnation to those who are in Christ Jesus, who do not walk according to the flesh, but according to the Spirit.

ROMANS 8:1 NKJV

Black Clouds Begone

These days you don't have to be in court to watch the procedures. Through cable, television, movies, and the media, you can watch cases from your own home. At the end of the trial you'll see the defendant stand as the verdict is read. Often it is "Guilty as charged." The next stage is for the judge to give the sentence. After the judge pronounces the sentence—"Death by lethal injection," "Life imprisonment"—the accused, perhaps wrestling with self-hatred and inner recriminations, is led out of the courtroom.

No one looks forward to being judged in a court of law. Similarly, no person relishes the idea of standing before God and having his errors read. Guilt is a horrible thing. It makes you feel low, small, hated, and broken.

Romans 8:1 speaks volumes of hope to every woman who feels the cringe and crush of guilt and judgment. Even though you may not be accused in a court of law, guilt can still pronounce a judgment on your life and

> Jesus took your guilt away, got rid of it, destroyed it forever. You are acquitted and free.

make you feel miserable for hours, months, years. There is a great truth about guilt. Its black cloud no longer hovers over your head. No one in heaven accuses you. Jesus took your guilt away, got rid of it, destroyed it forever. You are acquitted and free. Your thoughts may accuse, but they are lies. Jesus freed you from guilt and self-hatred and gives you new thoughts and joys.

Do you want real freedom from guilt? Because of Jesus's death on the cross, you are no longer guilty. You are new, clean, and beautiful in his eyes. He doesn't judge you, so don't judge yourself. You are free to live in joy and peace.

Always be willing to listen and slow to speak. Do not become angry easily, because anger will not help you live the right kind of life God wants.

JAMES 1:19–20 NCV

Breaking Out of an Angry Episode

Every woman has felt anger—sometimes deep anger—over bad treatment, disobedient children, an insensitive husband. What might dispel the anger you feel? What truth can you turn to that will eliminate the bitterness in your soul?

James gave you this most important verse about anger. He offered three pertinent guidelines to anyone who feels the sting of inner anger. First, be willing to listen. Listening gives the person you're angry with a chance to make a defense, or at least to explain his or her actions. But if you jump all over him before you've given him a hearing, how will you know if your anger is justified? Listen. Perhaps a solution will be apparent, or perhaps you will find that a miscommunication has occurred. If you are willing to listen to the other person, he or she will be more likely to listen to your perspective.

> **If you are willing to listen to the other person, he or she will be more likely to listen to your perspective.**

Second, be "slow to speak." James meant for you to think, to meditate, to look at the situation from all angles. Don't jump to conclusions and berate your opponent. Consider the situation in depth before you respond. Third, remain "slow to anger." Okay, you've listened, thought it all through, but you're still angry. What is the answer? Calm yourself. Dampen the anger. Don't speak harshly. Seek self-control with the help of God's Spirit.

~*

If you follow James's practical steps when you feel angry, you will never say things you regret or cause more pain because of your reaction.

We know that all things work together for good to those who love God, to those who are the called according to His purpose.

ROMANS 8:28 NKJV

Since God has shown us great mercy, I beg you to offer your lives as a living sacrifice to him. Your offering must be only for God and pleasing to him, which is the spiritual way for you to worship.

ROMANS 12:1 NCV

Your Greatest Sacrifice

An old story pictures a young, recently converted woman waking up in the morning. As her eyes open and her mind clears, she repeats a little ceremony she does every morning. Without getting out of bed, she prays: "This bed is the altar; I am the sacrifice. I give my life to you this day, O God, all of today. Use me as you wish. I am your servant." With those words, she gets up, dresses, and goes into her day ready to serve God and to respond when she hears his voice in her heart.

As a servant of God, think of yourself as a sacrifice to him. Paul wrote to the Roman believers to encourage them to give themselves to God in this way. Personal sacrifice is a voluntary thing; God doesn't demand it from you. Paul merely encouraged the Romans to take this step, and his words encourage you to do the same—every day, if necessary. This is the best way to worship God, by giving yourself to him.

> **Personal sacrifice is a voluntary thing; God doesn't demand it from you.**

You make this sacrifice through a simple choice: choose to tell God you want him to use you for his purposes. Ask him to work in your life, to lead you, and to empower you. You may not notice the difference immediately, but as you live for him day by day you will see it. New energy and enthusiasm will flood your heart. A great desire to get involved in his work in the world will grip you.

Give yourself up to God's leading, will, and purpose. This is the truest and surest route to the blessings he plans to give you in this life.

Do not be conformed to this world, but be transformed by the renewing of your mind, that you may prove what is that good and acceptable and perfect will of God.

ROMANS 12:2 NKJV

Transformed

"I want to be a better person." "I wish I wouldn't react that way all the time." "I can't stop myself. It just happens, and then I feel wretched." Most women have said such words and want desperately to be different than they are. Bad habits, stress reactions, and harsh responses make women feel guilty. But you can overcome such character traits.

God can make you a new and different person, and he can tame that tiger in your soul. Notice what Paul said in his letter to the Romans. He said you shouldn't be conformed to or in harmony with the world. Rather, you should be "trans-

formed by the renewing of your mind." That "renewing" is the crucial idea here. You are renewed by giving your life—your habits, your thoughts, your words—over to God. You commit yourself to listening to him and seeking what he wants for you.

> **You are renewed by giving your life—your habits, your thoughts, your words—over to God.**

Gradually, day by day, God's Spirit works in your heart to change you.

A woman who lived in an arid climate wanted to grow grass in her yard. But it rained rarely. She planted the seeds, but they never grew, except in one place. The little patch of ground outside her kitchen window grew lush grass. What was the difference? Every day, she doused that part of her yard with the dishwater.

Dousing your mind with Bible knowledge, talking to God, and listening for his voice will transform you. Like that little patch of grass, you will grow a renewed mind that loves the good and does right.

Your word is like a lamp for my feet and a light for my path.

PSALM 119:105 NCV

The Light on the Path

Sometimes everyone comes at you all at once with demands, and you feel overwhelmed. The women's group at church is telling you that you need to help missionaries. The local schools say you need to be involved in helping school kids—whether you have any or not. The nonprofit organizations and ministries call on you to volunteer. Your employer asks you to spend extra time at the office.

Watchdog groups beg you to stand for their causes. Pretty soon, all those directives can make a woman feel like a spinning top.

Guidance is a critical part of following Jesus. He wants you to know what he desires you to do. He wants you to include him in the decisions you make in your life. The way to do this is through the Bible. The Bible is like a lamp. It lights up the path ahead so you can see.

> **The Bible is like a lamp. It lights up the path ahead so you can see.**

The Bible is like a flashlight or a lantern that lights up only a few feet ahead, but it will light up enough of your road to enable you to see God's purpose for you each day. Pray first, and then reach for your Bible. Talk to God about the demands on your life, and ask for his help. God will use the Bible to show you where you need to go, and the Bible will give you wisdom to make the right choices.

Sometimes you will have a tough time discerning what path to take. Through the Bible, you will gain the insight and wisdom needed to make good, right decisions. Let the light of its truth direct *your* path.

God is Spirit, and those who worship Him must worship in spirit and truth.

JOHN 4:24 NKJV

True Worship

A young woman sways to praise music in a large church sanctuary. In the front row, a middle-aged woman gets out of her seat, turns, and kneels in the pew with her head in her hands to pray. In the middle of the sanctuary, another woman sits, her eyes open, her lips moving, but with no words coming out.

Clearly, all three women could be worshiping God in ways that please God. What they show is that it isn't the outward position—kneeling, standing, sitting, dancing—or the exuberance of the expression. Rather the heart connection is what counts.

Worship is the highest expression of human love and devotion to God. Jesus's words in John 4:24 reveal that worship most truly occurs when your spirit connects with God's Spirit, when the real you meets the real him and honors him for his love, grace and sacrifice. You can do that in any position, in any place, at any time, and with any attitude. Most people occasionally feel that their worship is little more than going through motions. Ask God to work in you his real, Spirit-to-spirit worship. Ask the Spirit of God to guide you. As you grow and learn, worship will become a blessed reality and a part of your life that you could never forget, overlook, or skip.

> **Worship is the highest expression of human love and devotion to God.**

Real, intimate worship is worth the effort to develop in your life.

Your attitude should be the same that Christ Jesus had. Though he was God, he did not demand and cling to his rights as God. He made himself nothing; he took the humble position of a slave and appeared in human form. And in human form he obediently humbled himself even further by dying a criminal's death on a cross.

PHILIPPIANS 2:5–8 NLT

Giving Up the Rights

Most people think they have rights: the right to live where they want; the right to do as they please; the right to read and view whatever entertainments they wish; the right to life, liberty, and the pursuit of happiness. These are all human ways of saying, "I'm free. I can do what I want. No one is stopping me." But rights are not the big issue to God. God wants to know how obedient you are to his Word and to his Spirit.

If you think obedience is too tough a rule, consider Jesus. He is royalty. He created the universe. Every person will one day bow the knee to him. Yet when he lived in this world, his attitude was one of abject obedience. He obeyed God the Father even to the point of an excruciating death on a cross.

> **You are in good company when you seek to obey God.**

God wants you to obey even when it involves pain. He desires that you obey even if it isn't in your self-interest. He longs that you learn to obey no matter what the cost. That's how Jesus obeyed. Think of the many women in the Bible who obeyed God: Rahab, Ruth, Deborah, the Virgin Mary, Mary the sister of Lazarus, Mary Magdalene. You are in good company when you seek to obey God.

God values your obedience so much that he promises to exalt every person who obeys, as Jesus did, in his new heavens and earth. Go ahead and obey him — it is worth it.

To them God willed to make known what are the riches of the glory of this mystery among the Gentiles: which is Christ in you, the hope of glory.

COLOSSIANS 1:27 NKJV

The Hope of Glory

In the Old Testament, the word *glory* is from the Hebrew word *kabod*. This word can be translated as, among other things, "weight, weightiness, greatness, glory." To be a woman with great weight is not something most women desire. But this is not about physical girth. When the Hebrews spoke of God's glory, they meant his great weight in the eyes of people. He mattered more than anyone else. He possessed ultimate and eternal significance as a person.

Perhaps you have heard the expression "He throws his weight around." Or you've discussed a "heavy issue" like God's sovereignty. Or maybe you have heard that someone "spoke with gravity." Such terms are used to describe important people who possess tremendous power or charac-ter, or to describe issues that can't eas-ily be sloughed off. Ultimately, that is the meaning of *glory*: "significance."

> **Through faith in Jesus, you become a person of significance, importance, magnitude.**

The one who possesses the most glory has the greatest weight or significance.

Colossians 1:27 stands out as one of those verses of tremendous significance for it proclaims that through faith in Jesus the "hope of glory" is gained. How does that happen? Through faith in Jesus, you become a person of significance, importance, magnitude. Perhaps you have felt that you don't count or that you aren't an important person to God. Push away such thoughts. If you are following Jesus, you are sig-nificant.

⸺⁂⸺

One day God will elevate you in the eyes of all creation as one of his magnificent subjects. That is the true hope of glory.

Do not be overcome by evil, but overcome evil with good.

ROMANS 12:21 NKJV

Overcoming Evil

Eileen was a natural for promotion when an administrative assistant position opened. She was a hard worker; she was capable, and she had seniority. Everyone in the office was shocked when a relatively new staff member got the job instead of Eileen.

Eileen soon learned the details. The new coworker had campaigned for the position. She'd subtly criticized Eileen—and even lied—to bosses who didn't know Eileen that well. And the coworker's schemes had worked. Eileen was devastated as she watched the new administrative assistant flaunt the position she wasn't qualified to hold.

Eileen faced the real test one day when she walked into a break room and found the administrative assistant crying. Eileen started to leave, thinking of the dishonesty, the manipulation, and all the things this woman had done to get her position. But Eileen felt compelled to ask

> When you think evil is conquering you, you can take the upper hand by refusing to sink to its level.

what was wrong. As she sat and listened to her coworker's woes, she found compassion and forgiveness building in her heart.

Evil can take many forms in your life and can threaten to overwhelm you. When you think evil is conquering you, take the upper hand by refusing to sink to its level. With God's help, you can conquer the bad in your life and counter it with good. Whatever form evil may take in your life, God promises that you don't have to let its power overwhelm you.

Conquer problems, tough situations, and hard circumstances by doing good. As you act kindly and wisely, God uses you to make a dent in the overall difficulties in this world.

The LORD is constantly watching everyone, and he gives strength to those who faithfully obey him.

2 CHRONICLES 16:9 CEV

The Eye in the Sky

Some cities are implementing a new program at traffic lights. Cameras at intersections take pictures of the license plates of cars running red lights. Then the car owners automatically get tickets in the mail. The message from the police force is clear: "We're watching you." The same thing is true in many department and grocery stores—surveillance cameras keep an electronic eye on customers.

As powerful as electronic eyes are, they're nothing compared with God. If you were raised in church, you probably know a few songs about God's eyes being on you. It would be easy to get into the frame of mind that God is like a traffic cop or surveillance camera—just waiting to catch you being bad. Entertainer Mark Lowry counters this attitude. He tells his audiences that God doesn't watch his people to see if he can catch them doing wrong; he watches because he is in love with his people. "God's eyes are constantly on you," Lowry exclaims.

> God watches you so he can find just the right ways to use your faithful heart and committed outlook in his world.

"He can't take his eyes off you because he loves you so much."

God is watching. But not to condemn. God's eyes go throughout the world, and he looks for those with character and faithfulness. God watches you so he can find just the right ways to use your faithful heart and committed outlook in his world. He could do the job alone, but he wants to employ you to help.

~♨

God's eyes are watching you today. As he sees you obeying him, he'll continue to fill your life with his strength, power, and love.

Who can find a virtuous wife? For her worth is far above rubies. The heart of her husband safely trusts her; so he will have no lack of gain.

PROVERBS 31:10–11 NKJV

Becoming a Trusted Woman

Trust is an elusive thing. It's frustrating to try to regain someone's trust when you've lost it. Trust is a paramount issue of life. Without trust in its leaders, a nation sinks into civil war. Without trust in his parents, a child might go his own way and end up in great trouble. Without trust in your faith, you risk doubt. When you don't trust your friends, you risk loneliness. When you don't trust your spouse, you're worried and afraid. You are anxious that the marital relationship will be broken. Trust is vital.

Every woman wants her husband to trust her, to rely upon her as faithful and true. But such trust doesn't come easily. How does a woman become trusted by the one who is nearest and dearest to her? Here are a few thoughts. One, she keeps her word.

> Every woman wants her husband to trust her, to rely upon her as faithful and true. But such trust doesn't come easily.

When she makes a promise, she fulfills it. Always. Her husband knows her word is good. Two, she is there when he needs her. When her husband is hurting, she is ready to listen as long as it takes, and she is ready to comfort him. When he's in trouble, she defends him. She is his ally. And three, she can be counted on. As they say, "When the chips are down, she's down there with him." She would never brush him off.

Do your best to keep the trust strong in your relationship. Then you'll enjoy one of God's greatest blessings on earth — a great marital relationship.

A gentle answer turns away wrath, but a harsh word stirs up anger.

PROVERBS 15:1 NASB

The Spiral Stopper

Disagreements often go like this: "Why didn't you take the trash out?" "Oh, I forgot." "You forget everything." "No, I don't. I remembered—" "No, you're the most forgetful person I ever met." "You're just mean." "Oh, you want to see mean?" And on and on it goes.

Arguments often start over minor issues—someone forgot to do what he promised, or someone forgot to say she'd be a little late, or someone did or didn't do something else—but these issues can escalate from the inconsequential into accusations, put-downs, and painful words that both parties remember long and regret at their leisure. There is a way to break that spiral and to keep an argument from becoming nasty.

Proverbs 15:1 ranks high among the all-time great solutions for women who can't seem to end the quarrel spiral. The solution is to answer gently, even if it is easier to speak defensively. A gentle answer can bring an argument to an abrupt halt. Instead of shooting a comeback that stings, say something gentle; perhaps even agree with the

> **A gentle answer can bring an argument to an abrupt halt.**

other person. "I'm sorry." "I'll try to do better." "Please forgive me." Such mild answers defuse an argument and bring it to a halt. Even if your antagonist responds with something like "You always say that," keep speaking those easygoing sentences. Stifle a mean comeback. Eventually this tactic will work.

⟶⁓

The gentle response can cool off a hot situation and turn it into a time to learn, to grow, and to better understand others. A peacemaker always wins God's blessing.

If any of you needs wisdom, you should ask God for it. He is generous and enjoys giving to all people, so he will give you wisdom.

JAMES 1:5 NCV

The One-Stop Wisdom Source

Women need friends, and it helps to have friends for different aspects of life. For instance, one of Susan's closest friends is Rhonda. After years of being a career woman, Susan got married and had kids. Rhonda was raising four kids during all those years when Susan was in an office. So when Susan needed parenting advice, she called on Rhonda. Susan found Rhonda to be a great sounding board and a good source of wisdom on family matters. A few years later, Rhonda decided to reenter the work force she'd been out of for twenty years. This time, at odd moments during the day, Susan's phone would ring. Rhonda would call, asking how to deal with office politics.

> **God knows everything there is to know about all areas of your life.**

It is wonderful to have friends who can give you wisdom in various areas of your life. They can give you reassurance and comfort for the challenges you face. But even your wisest friends can help you only so much. Their wisdom is limited. But God's wisdom isn't. God knows everything there is to know about all areas of your life. And he wants to pass his wisdom on to you. He is willing to share his intellectual and spiritual wealth with you.

God is all-wise, and God shares that wisdom with you. God promises that if you ask him to help, he won't lecture, scold, or think less of you.

A woman is wise to call in a consultant for matters she can't handle—especially the Divine Consultant.

Where God's love is, there is no fear, because God's perfect love drives out fear. It is punishment that makes a person fear, so love is not made perfect in the person who fears.

1 JOHN 4:18 NCV

The Antidote for Fear

Fear can strike at any time. You might be driving down the highway when a truck suddenly veers into your path. Only a quick reaction and a swerve can save you from destruction. *Whew!* Just a few seconds made a difference. How your heart pounds and your pulse races when something like that happens.

Still, other fears can seem bigger, more threatening, and there is no end to them: fear that someone you care about will die, fear that a son or a daughter will go wrong, fear that you will lose your job, fear that you'll lose your health, fear that you'll lose your investments, fear that you will lose your husband or your best friend or another loved one.

You needn't live a life of fear. Bad things will always happen in this world. No one can control bad things, and your problem may not be fixed immediately. But fear—sitting in a room and worrying, fretting over what might happen, living with deep anxiety—can be dealt with. Undoubtedly, the most important verse for a woman who lives with fear is 1 John 4:18.

> **God has the power to deal with whatever causes you fear.**

Love drives fear away, and knowing you are loved perfectly means you needn't be afraid of anyone or anything. The God who loves you also rules over everyone else. God has the power to deal with whatever causes you fear, and you can place your confidence in him.

When you know you are loved, and when you respond to others with love, fear disappears. When you know you are loved, God's grace, power, and presence embrace you. You know you are always in God's hands of love.

If any of you needs wisdom, you should ask God for it. He is generous and enjoys giving to all people, so he will give you wisdom.

JAMES 1:5 NCV

The LORD says, "My thoughts are not like your thoughts. Your ways are not like my ways. Just as the heavens are higher than the earth, so are my ways higher than your ways and my thoughts higher than your thoughts."

ISAIAH 55:8–9 NCV

Who Can Understand God?

Experience is wonderful. Teaching a young teen to drive will remind you of that fact. So will training an inexperienced new employee.

Experience is a terrific tool. But no matter how much experience, knowledge, and understanding you have about life, you, and all humans, still fall way short of God. He is on a plane higher than mortals can even fathom. His thoughts aren't the same as yours. Sometimes people get caught in the trap of thinking that God is like them—only smarter. But a couple of verses in Isaiah say that the best of human brains aren't even on the same playing field as God. God isn't just smarter; his thinking is beyond anything humans are capable of. If women are mentally from Venus

> God promises to come through in your life in a way that will work for you and satisfy you.

and men are mentally from Mars, well, then God is from heaven.

For you as a woman, this means that when your path appears blocked, God sees a way. When you see the finite world around you and the challenges it brings, God sees beyond them. God sees far beyond your world. God is totally superior to humans. You can trust God, and you can turn to him when you need someone bigger, someone whose knowledge is all-encompassing. God promises to come through in your life in a way that will work for you and satisfy you.

When you don't know what decision to make, when you feel stymied or oppressed, remember God. He can carve a path through that problem.

Seek first the kingdom of God and His righteousness, and all these things shall be added to you.

MATTHEW 6:33 NKJV

First Things First

Dreams have a variety of forms. Your dream could take the form of a personally designed house on several acres in a rural setting, of getting through college with at least a 3.75 GPA, or of landing a coveted job with a high salary, amazing perks, and a company car.

Nothing is wrong with dreaming. God wants you to dream and dream big. God has plans to knock your socks off with the blessings he wants to give you, both in this world and the next. But dreams also have their place.

Matthew 6:33 reveals the kind of prioritizing that God desires you to make in placing your dreams in context. In Jesus's Sermon on the Mount, he clinched the issue of where your priorities should be. He told his listeners that they all needed food, drink, and clothing, and that they worried about these things constantly. He told them how they could make sure they got them—by giving priority to God's kingdom and God's work in the world.

> God has plans to knock your socks off with the blessings he wants to give you, both in this world and the next.

Seeking God's kingdom means many things to many people. But as a start, be sure you become involved in a church and reach out to your neighbors with the gospel. Write that letter to the editor on the local issues important to you as a woman of faith. At the same time, let God know about your dreams, hopes, needs, concerns. He will supply them as you work with and for him.

When you pour yourself into God's concerns, you discover that God gives you the things you most desire and need. Trust him to come through for you, and keep your eyes on the priority.

In everything give thanks; for this is the will of God in Christ Jesus for you.

1 THESSALONIANS 5:18 NKJV

Don't Forget to Say Thanks

Drew was just a little guy. He wasn't in school yet, but he was old enough to know the universal truth: when the doctor gives you a shot, it hurts. Pam, his mom, prepared him for his visit to the doctor by explaining immunizations—how they hurt a little but in the long run they can keep people from getting ill. Instead of the shot hurting Drew, she explained, the shot would actually be helping Drew. Little Drew remembered his mom's words as he sat on the table. He squeezed his blue eyes shut as the doctor approached. Tears rolled down his cheeks when he felt the prick of one needle, then another. Little Drew quietly sobbed the whole time, while his little voice rang out, "Thank you. Thank you for making me better."

Sometimes life is great. You're sailing along, enjoying the breeze of good times. Everything is wonderful. At those times it's easy to say, "Thank

> **Thank God in all circumstances, the good times and the not-so-great ones.**

you, Lord. Thank you for this terrific life and everything you've done for me." When life is good, it is important to realize just who has provided that great life and all those blessings.

Life isn't always ideal. Sickness, trials, and discouragement sometimes seem to dog you. Nevertheless, thank God in all circumstances, the good times and the not-so-great ones. Like little Drew, tears might be rolling down your cheeks as you say, "Thank you, God. Thank you."

When you thank God, even through pain, amazing things happen in your heart. Somehow you find the grace and courage to be glad that God is still God—when life is good, and when it isn't.

Trust in the LORD with all your heart, and lean not on your own understanding; in all your ways acknowledge Him, and He shall direct your paths.

PROVERBS 3:5–6 NKJV

Be Wary of Your Perceptions

These famous and important words—to trust in the Lord—speak to nearly any situation a woman can encounter. You might be worried about a new job you've accepted or one you've rejected. Trust in the Lord. You may be concerned about your mother's surgery and her recovery. Trust in the Lord, and don't depend on your own understanding of things. You may wonder why your boss repeatedly questions your decisions. The verse says it all: seek God's will and trust him. Follow God, and he'll lead you.

This verse functions as the do-it-all repair kit of spiritual living. It can be used in many situations and offers wisdom that is unparalleled by anything you might hear from the rest of the world. But for a moment, take a look at that little phrase, "lean not on your own understanding."

When you encounter a circumstance that seems tough to resolve, you will naturally lean on your own perception of things. You might try to guess your boss's motives. Or your common sense may tell you to go one way, the wrong way. This verse tells you to instead listen for God's directions. Trust him. Refuse to think all is lost because your

> **Seek God's will, and trust him. Follow him, and he will lead you.**

mind tells you that. Rely on God, and he will bring you through. Consider memorizing Proverbs 3:5–6. It is the ultimate prescription for inner peace.

~ॐ

Trust God, and refuse to listen to what your brain is telling you; seek God always, and he will open up to you the way.

To me, to live is Christ, and to die is gain.

PHILIPPIANS 1:21 NKJV

Death to Life

Many people fear death. They worry that it could be painful, or extended. For humans, death is the ultimate enemy none of us can defeat on this earth. All religions in some way try to deal with the problem of death, making great promises about an afterlife or about another chance in this life. Christianity alone possesses the only One who has beaten death: Jesus. When Jesus rose from the dead after being crucified, he destroyed the devil's final bastion of power over humankind. Jesus proclaimed that anyone who believed in him would also defeat death.

The apostle Paul faced death many times. Romans, Pharisees, and emperors threatened him. But he never gave in, and he never feared. While Paul lived on earth, he would know and experience Jesus all the more. And if he died, he would go to the presence of Jesus and live with him forever. For Paul, death was a chance to gain even more of what he had on earth, but with one difference: he would never have to die again.

> **Jesus promises that death is the doorway to the adventure of an eternity.**

Perhaps you have a great fear of death. Push those thoughts away. Jesus promises that death is the doorway to the adventure of an eternity. Death holds no scary monsters or demons. Death will be the ultimate journey of joy.

Paul gave this antidote for women of all ages: live for Jesus. Do all you can to please him. That way, when the end comes, it will be a welcome move from the pains of this world to the glories of the next.

I say to you, her sins, which are many, are forgiven, for she loved much. But to whom little is forgiven, the same loves little.

LUKE 7:47 NKJV

A Whole Lot of Love

Most women want to love God with all their souls. Some people may wonder, though, how this is possible when so many other responsibilities intrude on their relationship with God. A relevant verse gives us a clue: in the story told in Luke 7, Jesus dined at the house of a Pharisee. When Jesus went into the house, no one washed his feet or anointed him, as was the custom. A prostitute learned that Jesus had come, and she went to the house, anointing Jesus with an expensive perfume.

The Pharisee wondered how Jesus could allow this, the woman being a prostitute. Jesus then told a parable about forgiveness, making the point that when you realize how much you are forgiven, you love God greatly. But when you are forgiven little, you love little.

If you hurt someone badly by word or deed and then go to them to ask for forgiveness, that person's forgiveness means a great deal to you. Often he becomes an even better friend to you. Your hurt produced great love.

> When you realize how much you are forgiven, you love God greatly. But when you are forgiven little, you love little.

The woman who went to Jesus was a known prostitute. She gave her body to be used for the sexual pleasure of others. In her culture, that was considered a great wrong. But Jesus didn't mean that only prostitutes could appreciate real forgiveness. Their errors, after all, were no greater than other's. A tart tongue can hurt many people. Cheating, stealing, hating, racism, spreading rumors—all these are terrible acts that the Bible condemns.

Look at the failings in your life. Most people can't count the errors and hurts they've caused. But God forgives you for all of them. When you realize how much God forgives, your love for him will grow.

Whatever things were written before were written for our learning, that we through the patience and comfort of the Scriptures might have hope.

ROMANS 15:4 NKJV

Comfort Food Comes from a Warm Bible

"At Lidia's, comfort food comes from a warm, cast-iron skillet," the article advertised. Lidia's, a restaurant located in scattered cities in the United States, offers comfort cooking from an Italian perspective. Most women have some sort of favorite comfort food: chocolate, fries, apple pie, macaroni, fried chicken, or even, as Lidia's offers, favorite recipes their moms used to cook, such as lasagna or ravioli. Most comfort foods tend not to be so great as far as calories or fat grams go, but they sure can give an emotional boost.

Of course, eating isn't the outlet for every woman when she's blue. Some women go to "comfort places"—a favorite store, a library, a coffee shop, a park. Other women reread favorite books or watch chick flicks. Still others get together with good friends to spill out hopes and needs. And many women turn to the Bible for comfort. The

> **The Bible is referred to as "food" for its readers' spirits and souls.**

Bible is referred to as "food" for its readers' spirits and souls. Now that's real comfort food.

Romans 15:4 reminds readers that the Bible was given to you for your benefit. The Bible is God's letter to you. You can learn and receive hope through reading the words of the Bible—words of encouragement, hope, companionship, and advice for your whole life—even for those times when you feel like singing the blues.

Ingest the Bible. Read it, memorize it, and study it, and you'll find plenty of comfort for your own soul—comfort you won't have to go to Lidia's or your refrigerator to get.

She was in bitterness of soul, and prayed to the LORD and wept in anguish.

1 SAMUEL 1:10 NKJV

Honest with God

Every woman grows up with dreams and expectations. Hannah was no different. In her era and culture, women were valued for their ability to produce children. So Hannah had probably grown up dreaming of the children she'd raise and love and call her own. Life hadn't turned out as Hannah had expected. Year after year, she remained barren. She had a husband who adored her, but her dreams of children hadn't come true. Over the years, the pain of life not turning out the way she expected apparently brought some bitterness into Hannah's soul. That was her frame of mind when she visited the temple and began to pray. As she silently talked to God, she didn't hide her feelings. She let her tears and her emotions pour out.

Many women, like Hannah, face unfulfilled dreams and disappointments. For whatever reasons, their lives aren't turning out as they expected. That kind of discouragement can gnaw at a woman's heart. Often when a woman's heart is hurting, she's tempted to avoid God but continue to act as if everything is okay.

> **When you face a disappointment—whether it is a long-term heartache or a brief pain—know that God cares.**

When you face a disappointment—whether it is a long-term heartache or a brief pain—know that God cares. He understands your feelings. You can follow Hannah's example by going to God and pouring your heart out before him. Be as intense as you want. Go to him with an honest heart, no matter what feelings you have.

Never hold anything back from God when you're talking to him. Like Hannah, enjoy having a relationship with God so free that you can talk about anything.

If you then, being evil, know how to give good gifts to your children, how much more will your Father who is in heaven give good things to those who ask Him!

MATTHEW 7:11 NKJV

The Best Dad Ever

Walk into most art museums, and somewhere you'll probably find a tender painting of a mother and child or maybe a study of a father and son, popular subjects in the art world. The parental relationship is the basis of all earthly relationships.

Though many family relationships are imperfect, the love a parent has for a child can be the most giving, sacrificial relationship that exists. Think about the ideal parent and child relationship. Mothers and fathers pour out time, energy, and money to take care of their children. They'd give their lives to protect their children. Ideal parents deal with each of their children on a personalized level, catering teaching and training to the style that most effectively helps each child. Parents help kids dream. They want the best for their children, but they also want their off-

> **The parental relationship is the basis of all earthly relationships.**

spring to be happy. Parents make themselves available to children to love them, comfort them, encourage them, and simply have a good time with them.

It is no wonder that many artists honor parents. And as much as parents love their children, it is truly staggering to realize that God loves his children even more than the most perfect earthly parents love their offspring. In every statement above, you could replace the word *parents* with *God* and the references to *children* with *your* name, and it would all be true.

God makes himself available to love you, comfort you, and encourage you. He's glad to be your divine Dad. Relish the closeness you can have with your heavenly Father.

G od began doing a good work in you, and I am sure he will continue it until it is finished when Jesus Christ comes again.

PHILIPPIANS 1:6 NCV

He Is Still Working On You

Jigsaw puzzles can be a terrific way to spend time. On the one hand, putting together the little pieces can be relaxing and intriguing. On the other hand, putting together jigsaw puzzles can be challenging and addictive. They can be so much fun that it's hard to stop working on them, even when you have other things to do. Watching as the design or photo on the jigsaw puzzle starts to take shape can be fascinating. Sometimes it's surprising to see how certain pieces fit together in places and ways you didn't expect.

Your journey on earth is like a jigsaw puzzle that God is continually working on. Here and there, he might put interesting pieces together in your life—pieces you don't expect or don't see how they could possibly fit in. But he works it all together. The great fact that Philippians 1:6 points out is that you don't have to work on your life alone—God takes responsibility for completing and perfecting you, too. For instance, if you're having

> **Your journey on earth is like a jigsaw puzzle that God is continually working on.**

problems with a certain temptation, you are not alone—God is helping you resist it. If you wonder if you'll ever get to a particular stage in your spiritual life, this verse reassures you that you will—because God is still working on you. One woman was afraid that she would mess up and not get to go to heaven. This verse reassured her that God intended to get her to her eternal destination unscathed.

You may not know what your life will turn out to look like, but God does. He is fitting all the pieces together until the beautiful masterpiece of you is completed. Keep in mind that as you work on your life, you don't work alone.

The LORD can control a king's mind as he controls a river; he can direct it as he pleases.

PROVERBS 21:1 NCV

In Control

Imagine you're at work and friends visit your house. If your home is "smart-wired," a security camera will flash a picture of who's at your front door on your computer screen at work. From work, you can invite your guests into your home, unlock the door, switch on the lights, get coffee brewing, and even start a CD playing to make them relaxed. All from the comforts of your office or other location. Being in control has never been so easy!

These "smart houses" may be new concepts for most people, but remote control is a practice that God has been incorporating for years! Proverbs 21:1 points out that God is in charge of the powers that be in our world. Those powers may not realize it. They may not even believe in God. But God still has the power to work in and through them to meet the needs of his people.

> **God has the power to work in and through leaders to meet the needs of his people.**

That doesn't mean everything every leader does will be good, but it still means God is in charge and can work through even the evil that men choose to do. For instance, even though believers in China are often persecuted and even killed for turning to God, China has more than seventy million people who love God and serve him — the more the persecution, the more people believe in God.

If you ever wonder what the world is coming to, rejoice that God is in charge. Pray for the country and its leaders, and trust God to work through them even when they don't know he is doing so.

You were once darkness, but now you are light in the Lord. Walk as children of light.

EPHESIANS 5:8 NKJV

The Tabloid Perspective

Enter most checkout lines, and you'll see them rimmed with gossip magazines and tabloid newspapers. Few people can resist the impulse to satisfy their curiosity. It's almost as if the tabloids reach out and grab you with their sensational headlines: "Elvis Alive in the CIA!"; "98-Year-Old Mummy Gives Birth to Twins!"; "Three-Headed Cow Is Really an Alien!" The tabloids and the surrounding magazines claim to expose the most personal and sometimes bizarre details of the lives of famous people. Impulse shoppers and tabloid fans purchase millions of copies a month. No one in public life is safe from the offensive sensationalism of these publications.

It seems as if this curiosity about others' lives has always been the trait of humanity. If exploitative presses had been in the Garden of Eden, papers would have announced "Adam and Eve on the Verge of Breakup!"; "Eve Eats the Apple!"; "A Swinging Night in the Serpent's Cove!"

> **Women are challenged to rise above the temptation to absorb and pass along juicy tidbits.**

The more dramatic the details, the more people want to hear. For some reason, humans love to pass along juicy tidbits. Women are challenged to rise above the temptation to absorb and pass along juicy tidbits. Set your sights in a new direction. Instead of discussing the latest immoral actions or wicked behavior of others, train yourself to focus on the positive elements in life and God's goodness.

Accept the challenge to avoid the tabloid perspective of life. When it comes to focusing on wickedness and immorality, go ahead, choose the high road. Set your mind on something else.

In everything give thanks;
for this is the will of God
in Christ Jesus for you.

1 THESSALONIANS 5:18 NKJV

*L*et us not grow weary while doing good, for in due season we shall reap if we do not lose heart.

GALATIANS 6:9 NKJV

Don't Lose Heart

The audience bristled with anticipation when the great English leader Sir Winston Churchill stepped to the podium. He looked over the crowd of graduating Oxford students and opened his mouth. Then he made what may be the shortest graduation speech in history: "Never give up." Some versions of this story say Churchill repeated those words three times, but it still probably qualifies for the shortest speech. Sir Winston apparently felt that was the most important message he could give to those who were embarking out into the world.

Galatians 6:9 goes into more detail, but it gives the same concept: never give up. In fact, Paul, the writer, encouraged readers not only to not give up, but to not get tired of doing good things. If you're human, once in a while, the blues will probably strike you—especially when you have been working hard and are physically or emotionally

> **Think of the end result. Don't concentrate on how you feel.**

tired. When you are blue, it is easy to want to just call it quits, to feel that your hard work is bringing no results.

Paul also gave a clue on how to find the courage, the strength, and the encouragement to go on: think of the end result. Don't concentrate on how you feel. Don't listen to any voice that tells you your hard work does no good. Just focus on your ultimate goal—like a runner who concentrates on the finish line during a race.

Don't be weary of doing what is good and right. Get some rest, ask God to help you, and keep going. The rewards will make your hard work worth it.

You should not stay away from the church meetings, as some are doing, but you should meet together and encourage each other. Do this even more as you see the day coming.

HEBREWS 10:25 NCV

The Oxygen of the Soul

Encouragement is the oxygen of the soul. Without oxygen, a human would die. With it, he lives. Pure oxygen, though, as you might have experienced in the hospital or another medical situation, is even stronger. Breathing that pure, simple substance can change a weak person into a strong one. You feel vitalized, uplifted, empowered.

Like oxygen, encouragement has the power to strengthen a flagging soul, heal a broken heart, and lift up a fallen outlook. Encouragement can come in many forms.

It might be a sincere compliment you give to a friend. It might be a note you write to thank a committee member for a task completed. It could be a pep talk you give to boost someone when her spirit is troubled. Or it might be a simple touch, a pat on the shoulder, the offer of a hand to help someone up when she has stumbled.

> When you take time to be with others, you find encouragement and help and hope to give to others and to yourself.

Encouragement comes in many forms. Encouragement often happens best in the context of fellowship or the gathering of people at church who believe as you do. Spend time with other godly women. Don't let your job and your family and all the other demands in your life isolate you. If something has to go, it's often the time you spend with other women in church, in women's programs, and in small get-togethers. When you take time to be with others, you find encouragement and help and hope to give to others and to yourself.

Fellowship that encourages is vital to survival. Get connected. Go to those meetings. Give and receive. You will find yourself lifting up and lifted up as if a cloud of oxygen were pouring into your lungs.

I also suffer these things; nevertheless I am not ashamed, for I know whom I have believed and am persuaded that He is able to keep what I have committed to Him until that Day.

2 TIMOTHY 1:12 NKJV

An Unboxed Faith

Mary Ruth keeps all of her special papers in a safe-deposit box at the bank. Whenever she wants to check her house deed, savings bonds, or other documents, she visits the bank and takes a look. Then she locks her box and entrusts it to the bank until the next time she wants to see those items. Besides papers, people keep jewelry, coins, and other valuables in safe-deposit boxes. People may leave their treasures there for years—or simply for a few months. Banks that offer this service have strict guidelines to guard their clients' personal property.

Just as you can entrust your personal possessions to the care of a bank, so also can you trust God with the intangibles in your life. God is fully trustworthy. Better than any bank, God holds on to whatever you give to

> Just as you can entrust your personal possessions to the care of a bank, so also can you trust God with the intangibles in your life.

him, whether emotions, thoughts, or even loved ones. Paul wrote this in a letter to his friend Timothy while Paul was in prison for his faith. Even in the face of being jailed because he believed in God, Paul still trusted God, and he encouraged Timothy to do the same.

You needn't lie awake at night worrying about your papers at the bank. And when you put something in God's hands, you can leave it there, knowing that God will take care of it—and you.

Entrust every aspect of your life—the hopes, dreams, and plans, as well as the concerns—to God today.

God, with his mercy, gave us this work
to do, so we don't give up.

2 CORINTHIANS 4:1 NCV

The Joys of Service

Go to your local elementary school on the day of a holiday party to check out the power of volunteerism in action. Chances are that you'll find the halls swarming with men and women who want to help. Or notice all the people behind the scenes at a community fund-raiser. Watch their faces, and you'll probably notice that they're having a great time.

Most women have areas of service in their lives. Whether it's at church or in the community, women tend to enjoy using their talents and skills to support events and organizations. When women get involved, things happen.

Women often have these opportunities to help others not because of chance but because God has given the situations to them. God has a purpose and a plan for your life. Sometimes those areas are part of that. Through serving, you can have an impact on the lives of men, children, and other women. Your commitment and kindness might be an example to someone else of how kind

> **When women get involved, things happen.**

and committed God is. Your willingness to help might show someone how God can help him or her. Seeing you using your abilities might encourage others to give their time and talent too.

Your involvement doesn't just benefit others. God gives you these areas to help through his mercy. You're not only doing good things for others, but you also reap profit. As you help others, you'll find that God rewards you in interesting, intriguing, and fun ways.

The next time you receive an opportunity to serve, enjoy it. Remember that it might be something God has placed in your life to improve your life and the lives of those around you.

We have this treasure from God, but we are like clay jars that hold the treasure. This shows that the great power is from God, not from us.

2 CORINTHIANS 4:7 NCV

The Treasure in You

If you want to go on a treasure hunt, look in your own mirror. According to Paul, the attractive woman looking back at you is full of value and hides a precious treasure. In the context of 2 Corinthians 4:7, the treasure Paul is talking about is Jesus. He is the treasure within you, and you are likened to a clay pot.

In the land and times of the Bible, clay pots were valuable to their owners. The pots may not have been as beautiful as a jeweled container, but the clay pots were useful and lasted long. They were ordinary, but they were invaluable for the tasks needed in the household. But no matter how valuable the jar, its contents were more valuable

> **Like all humans, you are fallible and are imperfect, but God still chose you.**

than the container. The value of the container lay in its ability to keep its contents safe.

Like a clay pot or jar, you are an ordinary tool, an everyday person. Jesus chose to live in you. Like all humans, you are fallible and are imperfect, but God still chose you. God is far wiser than any human — he created humans. But he chose to live inside mortals and to use believers on earth. He lives inside you. The glory comes because he lives inside his creation and works through every person to bring about great things in his world.

If you ever feel as boring as a clay jar, be glad. God chose to live in you and use you. It isn't *what* is on your outside that counts, but *who* is on your inside.

We have troubles all around us, but we are not defeated. We do not know what to do, but we do not give up the hope of living. We are persecuted, but God does not leave us. We are hurt sometimes, but we are not destroyed.

2 CORINTHIANS 4:8–9 NCV

Invincible

For years, Timex was one of the most popular watch brands. Perhaps you remember the famous Timex watch commercials. They showed scenes like a Timex being run over by a truck, going down rapids, facing almost every imaginable peril. But the Timex always came through—it might look a little battered, but it was still operational. For thirty-five years, the Timex theme was "Takes a lickin' and keeps on tickin'." Nothing could stop a Timex. It was advertised as being invincible.

That's also a theme you can adopt in your life. Paul, the man who wrote several books of the Bible, could have said it. He endured shipwrecks, beatings, imprisonment for his faith, and all sorts of tough times. But he kept living for God and talking about Jesus.

You may never hit tough times as a result of your faith. But at some time or another, you will probably hit some bumps in the road—that's part of life.

> You can remain emotionally, spiritually, and mentally victorious by reminding yourself that you have God's power on your side.

Although trying times may come in life, you can still emerge from them triumphant. Like that Timex watch, you may look a little battered, but you don't have to be beaten. You can remain emotionally, spiritually, and mentally victorious by reminding yourself that you have God's power on your side. Instead of focusing on the troubles, concentrate on the positives—on your ability to overcome the tough stuff with God's help.

God promises to be there with you to face the tough times. No matter what life throws at you, you can take the lickin' and keep on tickin'.

Our only goal is to please God whether we live here or there.

2 CORINTHIANS 5:9 NCV

Keeping the Main Thing the Main Thing

What a wonderful time this is for a woman to be alive. A woman today can enjoy so many things her mother, grandmothers, and great-grandmothers never even imagined. For instance, if you're a baby boomer, your mother might not have known how to drive a car. Or she might have been discouraged from having a career or going to college. Women today are free to pursue their dreams and interests while also enjoying a family and focusing on a home. Maybe no woman can ever have it all, but today's woman comes closer than ever.

While you have more freedom than your foremothers, you also tend to face more busyness. Even if you don't work outside the home or take college classes, schools, community organizations, and churches call on you to volunteer. If you have children, they're getting more homework than ever that requires your help. As the life expectancy increases, you may need to care for aging parents. You could probably add a few activities to those already mentioned.

> Maybe no woman can ever have it all, but today's woman comes closer than ever.

With all the activity and busyness, it's easy for a woman to lose focus in her life. It's normal to live in survival mode and not think about why you're doing what you're doing. It's easy to focus on activities and not think about God. Remember to keep the main thing the main thing, as one pastor puts it. God should be the main focus in your life. While you may need to keep busy, you still have to keep him front and center in your life.

Keep God as the main priority in your life, and you will find that he helps you meet all your other responsibilities. You will find a new sense of his presence in your life, along with a renewed vigor and guidance.

Christ accepted you, so you should accept each other, which will bring glory to God.

ROMANS 15:7 NCV

Through God's Eyes

When you look at the young woman, she sparkles. At twenty-nine years old, she is a beautiful woman who loves God. You might be surprised to learn she wasn't always that way. When she was a teenager and college-age, she frustrated most of the people who knew her by her determination to walk on the wild side of life. Drugs . . . promiscuity . . . she kept getting in deeper and deeper.

"For the longest time, I referred to her as a prodigal," says one of the women who works with and loves this young lady. "Then God urged me to see her as his child instead of as a prodigal rebel. That made all the difference. I started seeing her as he did—as a lovely child of God with promise and purpose. I still had to give her some doses of tough love, but I began to look beyond that stage and to picture her as the finished product, a woman after God's own heart. When I decided to do that, I stopped panicking and being depressed when I thought about her."

> When you're dealing with a difficult person, ask God to help you see him as he sees the person.

You may not have a prodigal teen or a fallen friend in your life, but most women at some time or another encounter someone who is a little difficult to deal with or is hard to like. It is sometimes tough to know what to do about these people. Romans 15:7 encourages you to accept others. When you're dealing with a difficult person, ask God to help you see him as he sees the person. Try to see him as if you were looking through God's eyes. He has a plan for that person's life and is still working on him.

Get in the habit of looking at others you know as masterpieces in the making. Imagine the wonderful things that God will do through them.

You are not the same as those who do not believe. So do not join yourselves to them. Good and bad do not belong together. Light and darkness cannot share together.

2 Corinthians 6:14 ncv

Go, Team

Kit and Michael enjoy inviting people to their home to play games. But they don't usually play on the same team. Kit chats during games and may not even notice when it's her turn. Michael, on the other hand, constantly plans strategy and watches others' moves. Kit's purpose is to have fun. Michael's focus is to win. Michael and Kit love each other, but they don't like to pair up.

In a sense, when you believe in God, it's like being on a team. You and other members of the team share similar goals and tend to focus on the same direction: obeying and following God while on earth. At times the goals you have may not be compatible with the focus of those who do not believe as you do. For instance, one man wanted to follow God with his whole life, but he teamed up with other businessmen to start a restaurant chain. His goal was to make a good living. His partners agreed but were more ruthless. They decided their restaurant should be known for sexual permissiveness. The man who wanted to follow God knew this philosophy was morally wrong. He was on a team that had a focus different from his, so he faced some tough decisions.

> For the closest friendships and relationships in life, a woman does best to stick with people who believe as she does.

You needn't avoid people who don't follow God. The Bible encourages those who serve God to have friendships and relationships with those who don't know God. However, for the closest friendships and relationships in life, a woman does best to stick with people who believe as she does.

Think about who the greatest influences are in your life. Don't hesitate to spend more time developing your closest relationships.

Is anything too hard for the LORD? No! I will return to you at the right time a year from now, and Sarah will have a son.

GENESIS 18:14 NCV

Nothing Too Hard for God

The average woman would be alarmed if angels showed up at her door and told her that even though she's long past childbearing years, she is going to have a baby. Sarah laughed. It wasn't that she didn't want to have a child. For most of her ninety or so years she'd tried to get pregnant. And this wasn't the first time God had sent the message that she was to become a mother. He'd said that before and nothing happened. So Sarah had tried to "help" God out by encouraging her servant girl to have a child with her husband, Abraham—a child she planned to raise. But Sarah's schemes to help fulfill God's promise ended up in a mess.

> Don't give up on God. His timing is not the same as yours.

After years had passed, God reminded Sarah and Abraham of his promise. Sarah's laughter indicated that she had given up on ever holding that baby. But the angels reminded her, "Is anything too hard for the LORD?"

Perhaps you believe that God promised you something, but you haven't seen the promise fulfilled. When that happens, it's tempting to try to finagle people and situations to make the desired results happen. And after disappointment, it's tempting to just give up on God. Don't give up on God. Keep your hope in him. His timing is not the same as yours.

What God promises, he will do. Put your faith into high gear and wait for him to act when everything is just right. Remember, nothing is impossible for God.

Don't worry about anything; instead, pray about everything; tell God your needs and don't forget to thank him for his answers. If you do this you will experience God's peace, which is far more wonderful than the human mind can understand. His peace will keep your thoughts and your hearts quiet and at rest as you trust in Christ Jesus.

PHILIPPIANS 4:6–7 TLB

Peace That Goes Soul-Deep

Peace. What a lovely word. Perhaps every woman envisions a different setting when she thinks about peace. One might think of a long, hot bubble bath. Another might think of a garden filled with fragrant flowers. Someone else might think of an afternoon with no children around. Whatever the vision, most women welcome moments of calmness and rest in their lives.

Peace goes deeper than external settings, though. Peace is an issue that goes all the way to the heart and soul—the inner core of your life. Here's the scoop on how to find total peace: take every concern and worry in your life to God in prayer. God is not just *willing* to listen to your cares, but he also *urges* you to talk to him about whatever is on your mind and heart.

> **When you talk to God about everything, something amazing happens.**

When you talk to God about everything, something amazing happens. Suddenly, you are filled with a peace that you didn't have before. You may not be able to understand why you feel so at rest. Sometimes this peace defies explanation because every logical bone in your body may tell you that you need to be concerned about an issue; but this calmness fills your soul, and instinctively you know God is in control. That is true peace.

⁓∭◎

God invites you to tell him everything that is on your mind. He will give you peace when you do.

D̲o not be drunk with wine, which will ruin you, but be filled with the Spirit.

EPHESIANS 5:18 NCV

The Friend Who Is Always Beside You

Many people who read the Bible stumble when they come across the command to be filled with the Spirit. Actually, being filled with the Spirit is a relatively simple concept, and it's one of the most exciting promises in the Bible. *Filled* means "to be led, controlled, empowered" by the Spirit of God. Becoming filled with the Spirit is not difficult—you don't have to go through any long processes. You become filled with the Spirit in your life simply by turning over your motivations and concerns to God. Through the Spirit who lives in you—a bit of a mystical concept, but a reality to those who invite him to take charge of their lives—you find that God gives you resources day by day to live as he wants you to. At times, you may be sitting in a doctor's office, in church, or at a meeting, and the Spirit will speak to you. The Spirit's voice might direct you in many areas—often with small

> **The filling of the Spirit is like having a friend right inside your mind and heart.**

details. He might suggest, *Make yourself a note to write a letter of encouragement to this person.* Or he may draw your attention to a certain person. *Go chat with that one. She looks like she needs to talk to someone.*

The filling of the Spirit is like having a friend right inside your mind and heart. He can speak, lead, encourage, or empower you at any time. At times, you won't even be aware that he is there because his gentle touch is so subtle.

Let the Spirit lead, guide, empower, and enfold you. Let him take full rein in your life. If you do, you will see God work through you in awesome ways.

We have this treasure
from God, but we are like
clay jars that hold the
treasure. This shows that
the great power is from
God, not from us.

2 Corinthians 4:7 NCV

Be strong in the Lord and in his great power.

EPHESIANS 6:10 NCV

The Power Booster

In 1980 Midway Games manufactured an arcade game called Pac-Man. It was an instant smash, and by 1982, Midway had turned out 300,000 Pac-Man games. The concept was simple—a little yellow ball called Pac-Man ran around the board eating dots and avoiding the monsters. The only time the monsters couldn't kill Pac-Man was when Pac-Man ate one of the four power pills, or energizers, on the board. When Pac-Man ate one of those, he was invincible and could eat the monsters. What a rush to try to get to one of the power pills before the monsters could get your frantic Pac-Man. Getting to the power pills at the right time was the key.

Not to trivialize Scripture or the human experience, but in a base sense, people are kind of like that little Pac-Man. You might be zooming around just taking care of all the dots of life you need to take care of. Then all of a sudden, you face a situation in which you're completely at the mercy of something barreling down on you. Like Pac-Man, you are incapable of dealing with the situation in your own power.

> You may not have a power pill to crunch on and make you invincible, but you have something better. You have God's power waiting at your disposal.

You may not have a power pill to crunch on and make you invincible, but you have something better. You have God's power waiting at your disposal. All you have to do is to call upon him, to lean on him, to depend on his abilities. Then you'll be stronger than the most powerful adversaries you may encounter.

The next time you need a power boost, turn to God. He'll build strength into your life that you never imagined you could possess.

Slaves, obey your masters here on earth with fear and respect and from a sincere heart, just as you obey Christ.

EPHESIANS 6:5 NCV

Changes in Your Life and in Your Heart

"I think my life is about to change, and actually, I'm excited about it." Jody didn't start out so pleased. For several years, she watched her coworker simper, slink, and practically seduce their boss. She watched her boss start favoring her coworker over other employees. With an office restructure ahead, Jody saw signs that her colleague would soon be her boss. "I think I'll take this as an opportunity to join another company," Jody said.

Most women have had to deal with a difficult boss or leader at some point. Unfortunately, not all women are like

Jody and can quit when this happens. When Paul wrote the letter to the Ephesians, some of the Ephesians faced a situation far worse than having a difficult boss. They were actually owned by another human—they were slaves. In their dire situation, they were encouraged to show respect nevertheless. They were to remember that with everything they said or did, they should keep serving as if they were serving Jesus himself.

> If you have a challenging boss, give him or her the respect the position deserves.

Women in any employed situation can draw heart from this story. If you have a challenging boss, give him or her the respect the position deserves. If you aren't really excited about one of your leaders at church or in another situation, keep serving as if you were serving God. Most women find that when they have this attitude, the leader notices—and often becomes more malleable. Even when the leader stays the same, the woman herself may change and become a better person all around.

Pray for your leaders. Be an example to them and reflect God's love in everything you do. Ask God to help you in this quest.

Every time you criticize someone, you condemn yourself. It takes one to know one. Judgmental criticism of others is a well-known way of escaping detection in your own crimes and misdemeanors.

ROMANS 2:1 MSG

A Look in the Mirror

Elizabeth prided herself on all the things she did right. She performed her job well, and received regular promotions and accolades for the work she did. She went to church every Sunday. She kept her apartment neat and tidy, everything in its place. She never let men try to take advantage of her, and she had an honest desire to remain pure until she got married.

Laurie, on the other hand, made every mistake possible. She was loose, freewheeling, and never saw a free drink she wouldn't slurp down. Every time Elizabeth saw Laurie hanging out in the lunchroom and gossiping, she prayed that the woman would be caught by the boss and reprimanded.

Then Elizabeth read Romans 2:1 about judging others. Elizabeth realized that she'd become like the Pharisees in the Bible. The Pharisees were people who were so religious that they were proud of their faith. The Pharisees were so religious that God's commands weren't enough for them, and they added a bunch of their own rules that they thought religious people should follow. Because they followed these rules, they thought

> **The Pharisees were so religious that God's commands weren't enough for them, and they added a bunch of their own rules that they thought religious people should follow.**

they were better than anyone else. The Pharisees didn't really love God; they tolerated him.

Elizabeth bowed her head in prayer and confessed her poor attitude to God. Immediately a new sense of freedom flooded her heart, and she realized Laurie was just another worker who had her own problems and difficulties.

It's hard not to judge. When you find yourself putting others down, take a look into your own life. Then act with mercy and understanding.

Because you have these blessings, do your best to add these things to your lives: to your faith, add goodness; and to your goodness, add knowledge.

2 PETER 1:5 NCV

Working on Your Masterpiece

In 1932, a carpenter began to use his off-season to make children's toys. Pretty soon, the toys were selling so well that he dropped the carpentry business. One of his creations is one of America's all-time favorite toys—something you probably played with when you were a child: LEGO construction toys. The object of LEGO is that you attach plastic bricks to other plastic bricks and keep adding more bricks to the previously laid bricks until you build a wonderful masterpiece.

What a good analogy of a woman's spiritual life. As a woman strives to be closer to God, and to be more like him, she is building. Her foundation is having a relationship with God as she places her faith in him. On top of her faith, a woman builds goodness—she develops qualities such as decency, morality, and kindness. To make her faith more well-rounded and effective, a woman adds knowledge—she studies the Bible and learns more about God.

> To make her faith more well-rounded and effective, a woman adds knowledge—she studies the Bible and learns more about God.

Building faith doesn't come automatically, so a person has to work at it sometimes. You can have fun as you look for ways to be examples of God's goodness here on earth. And you can enjoy learning more about God and his grace and his love for people. It might even be as rewarding and enjoyable as, well, as building something with LEGO bricks.

As you move through your life today, look for ways to build your faith. Have your own spiritual treasure hunt, looking for those blocks that will make you stronger and more beautiful than ever.

I will sprinkle clean water on you, and you shall be clean; I will cleanse you from all your filthiness and from all your idols. I will give you a new heart and put a new spirit within you; I will take the heart of stone out of your flesh and give you a heart of flesh.

EZEKIEL 36:25–26 NKJV

Completely New Inside

Reality TV has made a tremendous impact on viewers. It started with one quite successful show and then seemingly exploded into several viewer favorites. One show depicts house doctors who perform a complete makeover of the dilapidated house of someone who sees no other way of making his or her home a castle. The builders come in, raze the old house if necessary, and rebuild everything. It's a complete makeover, and in the end some happy homeowners have a whole new property to live in.

This is not just a TV show, but also a picture of what happens to people when God changes them from the inside out. Picture God giving a person a "new heart." God removes the hard, useless, willful, and disobedient heart and puts in its place a new model—healthy and beautiful, perfectly attuned to God and pliant.

> **God removes the hard, useless, disobedient heart and puts in its place a new model—healthy, beautiful, perfect.**

This heart wants to obey God, follow his commands, and live out his plans. It is completely devoted to God.

That's what happened to you when you first started walking toward God. Maybe you fought with addictions, bad habits, and wrong attitudes that you couldn't stop. But God offered you hope. He made you over from the inside out. You are still you, and your personality is intact. But the attitudes, ideas, outlooks, and thoughts that fill your mind are different, new, life-giving, and life-enhancing. You are a new person.

~⑩

No matter how much remodeling you need at any point, you can become new with God's presence and help. He changes people from the inside out.

As each one has received a gift, minister it to one another, as good stewards of the manifold grace of God.

1 PETER 4:10 NKJV

Receiving Gifts to Give

Imagine it's your birthday and you go into the kitchen where a number of gaily colored packages are stacked on the table. The packages are of all sizes and shapes, but you tear into them eagerly as the members of your family look on. The first one opened, you find a little necklace with a heart on it. It's pretty, but the heart has an inscription: "A discerning heart." You open another package, and in it you find another strange item—a little rocket. It also has an inscription: "Boosting others." Still others read "Teaching," "Helping others," and "Exhortation" (challenging others to be their best).

You continue going through the packages, and suddenly you realize these aren't standard birth-day gifts. They are spiritual gifts from heaven. On your spiritual birthday— when you started believing in God— God gave you spiritual gifts. The gifts are intangible, like the ability to

> On your spiritual birthday—when you started believing in God—God gave you spiritual gifts.

encourage or comfort, the power to teach effectively or preach, the talent for leading or giving or helping in spiritual ways. These are personal packages of abilities, talents, and powers that God gives every person who loves him, but the mix of gifts is individualized so that no two people are exactly alike. No one else can help others in exactly the same way you can. Your gifts help you serve others effectively.

⌐∭◡

God gave you gifts for the purpose of service. Use those gifts. Give the multifaceted goodness of God to others. God will give back to you his grace, love, and joy.

Control yourselves and be careful! The devil, your enemy, goes around like a roaring lion looking for someone to eat.

1 PETER 5:8 NCV

On Guard

Toddlers can be fun, whether they're your own or someone else's. Ruth is a typical eighteen-month-old. You can easily entertain her by saying, "Where's Ruthie?" Immediately she slaps both chubby hands over her bright blue eyes and hysterically giggles until you cry, "There she is." Ruth thinks that as long as she has her eyes covered and can't see you, that you can't see her either.

Sometimes women take this attitude about wrong things happening in the world. Some women tend to think if they ignore problems—such as the wrong things people do in society—that those problems will not touch their lives. Unfortunately, that's not true. The Bible says that wrongdoing, hatred, racism, and so many other wrongs are real. Satan may not be a character with a pitchfork, but he exists on a spiritual level and encourages humans to disobey God and act

> Some women tend to think if they ignore problems—such as the wrong things people do in society—that those problems will not touch their lives.

with bad intent. Like little Ruth shutting her eyes, you can pretend such spiritual enemies don't exist and don't have an influence in the world, but when you do that, that's usually when you're the most vulnerable to temptations to do wrong.

No one is above being tempted. In fact, everyone has areas in which they're more likely to succumb. Take an honest look at the areas of temptation you face. Set ways to guard yourself from giving in to temptation.

You can rise above temptation and evil. Start by looking it square in the face and acknowledging that it's there.

People who do not believe are living all around you and might say that you are doing wrong. Live such good lives that they will see the good things you do and will give glory to God on the day when Christ comes again.

1 PETER 2:12 NCV

Glimpses of a Good God

Kim's goal in life was to be a missionary. So she jumped at the chance to take a sabbatical from her job and to volunteer with a mission organization in India. Soon she was in her missionary country, and while there, she had the opportunity to visit the Home for the Dying in Calcutta that Mother Teresa founded. Imagine Kim's thrill when she met her hero, Mother Teresa. Kim's face glowed when she told her coworkers about it. It was still so unbelievable. "She kissed me, right there," Kim said in awe, pointing to a spot on her forehead.

Not only people who want to be missionaries think highly of Mother Teresa. No matter what the religious background, every-one can agree: Mother Teresa was an extraordinary person. She wasn't known for her wealth, or for the other things that normally bring fame. She became famous for being good—for caring about people and taking care of them. Mother Teresa mirrored God, and many people worldwide heard her words and saw her actions and caught glimpses of God.

> **Many people worldwide saw Mother Teresa's actions and caught glimpses of God.**

Like Mother Teresa, you can have an influence among the people who circle your life. Focus on living a good life, a life that shows compassion and love, a life that reveals such kindness and warmth that people can see peeks of God through you.

Take a look around you today. Find ways to express sweet-ness and warmth. Bring a bit of God's goodness into some-one else's life.

Submit to God. Resist the devil and he will flee from you.

JAMES 4:7 NKJV

Resisting

You're walking down the street along an outdoor mall. You promised yourself you wouldn't overspend today. Suddenly you pass a clothing store, and you see it: the perfect outfit. It's just your size, your color, and the absolute epitome of what you need right now. You are about to go in when you remember your promise. The outfit costs far more than you can spend.

You start to turn away when a strange man appears. He taps you on the shoulder and says, "You need it, darling. Why resist?" Reasons shoot into your brain, but he shakes his head. "Nonsense, my dear. You can put it on your credit card."

You are almost sucked in when you take a harder look at this man. You've heard that voice before. In your heart. It's the voice of the tempter, the enemy of God, the one the Bible calls Satan. With all your might, you give this being a shove, kick him in the shins, then turn around and walk off, calm, cool, and resurrected.

Believe it or not, temptation like this is real, for some more than others. The voice you hear in your head can be the enemy, seeking to deceive, trick, or goad you into doing things you know are not right. The way to handle such an attack is to remember James 4:7, a potent verse vitally important in the battle against

> You've heard that voice before. In your heart. It's the voice of the tempter, the enemy of God, the one the Bible calls Satan.

temptation. Resist the enemy. God will empower you. You may even quote the verse aloud, using it as a sword to cut the sneaky webs of the enemy.

~!!!

You may think the enticement to do wrong will never end, that you are trapped. But God assures you: if you resist temptation, Satan will flee.

These are the ways of the world: wanting to please our sinful selves, wanting the sinful things we see, and being too proud of what we have. None of these come from the Father, but all of them come from the world. The world and everything that people want in it are passing away, but the person who does what God wants lives forever.

1 JOHN 2:16–17 NCV

The Gotta-Have-It Test

At some time in your life, you've probably been asked a variation of this question: "If your house was on fire and you had three minutes to grab anything, what would you save?"

Perhaps every woman should ask herself that question periodically. It helps you center on what is really important in your life — what *you* know is truly a priority. Think about it now. What would you grab on your way out? Your purse? Your family pictures? Your new name-brand gadget? Every day plenty of people and companies bombard you with their ideas of what's important in your life. They'll tell you that you have to have a great car to show how powerful you are and to keep you comfortable. You have to have certain clothes so you can look great, and better yet, get rid of the imperfections you've always hated in your body—those things that make you different—

> In a world where you are bombarded by fabricated needs, it helps to keep your internal compass on the truth.

through simple surgical enhancements. Buy a fabulous home so you can impress the friends you don't have time to have over. You know the advertising and marketing routines.

In a world where you are bombarded by fabricated needs, it helps to keep your internal compass on the truth. Periodically assess your life and discern what's really valued in your life. And remember to invest in what you can take with you to heaven.

If your life ended tomorrow, think about what you'd take with you and what intangibles you would leave behind. Keep your life in perspective.

Brothers and sisters, do not be surprised when the people of the world hate you.

1 JOHN 3:13 NCV

Popularity Contest?

When Joy became a manager, she received lots of advice from other managers. She valued all of it, but she says the best advice she received was this: "Managing is not a popularity contest." She worked in a new business, where many young up-and-comers were employed. Getting them in line and keeping them focused took discipline and some-times a stern word or two. Many times in life you simply have to say or do things whether other people approve or not. Your responsibility supersedes your congeniality.

Maybe you have faced this with your faith and morals. When you are striving to live for God, others may not understand that. They may not understand why you feel some attitudes and actions are wrong and why you support other ones. The important thing is to focus on the reality of living for God in a world where he isn't a priority. It is your responsibility and your privilege to live for God despite social impediments or major differences of opinion.

> Do your best to be winsome and likable. But know that if you're living for or talking about God, you may see some arrows fly your way.

Of course, that doesn't give you a license to be abrasive. Do your best to be winsome and likable. Friendliness is a good thing. But know that if you're living for or talking about God, you may see some arrows fly your way. If so, then do what you have to do.

~*~

Keep living for God. If someone doesn't understand, just keep following what you believe—and ask God to open the other person's eyes.

Do all things without complaining and disputing.

PHILIPPIANS 2:14 NKJV

The Attitude Cleaner

Glenda took on a new attitude when she became a Christian. Instead of complaining about others as she used to do, she often said, "God isn't through with them yet." When before she might have run off into a stream of curses or sarcastic comments about someone's mistake, she now said things like "I guess God had a different idea about that one." And when things simply didn't go her way, she took the positive view and said, "Thanks, God. You're giving me something to think about" or "I hadn't thought about that, God."

Not everyone can have such an attitude overnight, but Philippians 2:14 points out the style of life God's followers should have: no grumbling, complaining, or put-downs. Instead, find words of praise, thanks, affirmation, and encouragement.

Some people say it is easier said than done, but the starting point is simply refusing to complain or criticize when things go wrong. Fill your mind with good thoughts, healthy thinking, and words that refresh. Memorize Scriptures

> **Fill your mind with good thoughts, healthy thinking, and words that refresh.**

that can drive out the grumbling. Turn yourself into the one who always has something good to say, rather than be someone who always grumbles or makes snide comments. God will help you. Ask God to get involved with your attitude, and you'll find him reminding you when such words try to get out of your mouth.

Someone once said, "If you don't have anything good to say, don't say anything." Maybe a variation will help: "If you don't have anything good to say, say something good anyway."

$\mathbf{B}$rothers and sisters, we ask you to appreciate those who work hard among you, who lead you in the Lord and teach you. Respect them with a very special love because of the work they do.

1 THESSALONIANS 5:12–13 NCV

Appreciation and Respect

When Ann became a teacher in her church, she was surprised at some of the comments kids gave her. One said, "I like the way you teach. You're interesting." Another commented, "You know, you really make it easy to understand. Thanks." And a third said, "Someone told me you were mean, but I think you're nice. And you're really fun to listen to."

Unknowingly, those kids were living out a vital truth of Scripture found in 1 Thessalonians: you should respect and appreciate those who lead you and teach you. For some teachers, it's rare to hear something positive about a lesson or idea they had. Many become discouraged and are ready to quit because they see so few results. But when kids like those in Ann's class affirm a teacher the way they did, you can bet he or she is raring to go to class each week.

> You have the power to let one of those nurturers know how much they put into your life.

Think about some of the great teachers and leaders you've had over the years. Maybe it is time to write that note or make that phone call or drop by with a gift to one or even several of the people who encouraged you and led you. You may be surprised at the response, which will undoubtedly be one of gratitude and joy. You have the power to let one of those nurturers know how much they put into your life. So tell them. Don't hold back.

Everyone needs affirmation and encouragement. Appreciation is something anyone can give anywhere, anytime. Go appreciate someone today.

With God's power working in us, God can do much, much more than anything we can ask or imagine.

EPHESIANS 3:20 NCV

You Can't Even Imagine It

Jan came home stunned by what she had heard that night. The speaker had challenged his listeners to start thinking big for God. At one point, he quoted the powerful Ephesians 3:20 and said, "If God told you that you could ask him to do anything in this world in the next year, what would you ask for?" Jan didn't know, but she found herself thinking seriously about it.

She began to think bigger and wider than she'd ever thought before. The news about the tsunami in Southeast

Asia had mobilized the world, and that was pretty big. But then she thought: *What about an outpouring of God's Spirit on those people? How about the involvement of many others in helping them?*

She began praying about that and other things. God soon led her to put wings to her prayers, and she got involved in a missions effort to Cambodia. She flew halfway around the world and helped those poor people start a fishing industry. It was miraculous. Many Cambodians became believers in

> God wants you to try to imagine greater things for him to do than ever before.

Jesus, and fast friendships were formed that Jan knew would last forever.

Don't let anyone tell you that thinking big is not biblical. God wants you to try to imagine greater things for him to do than ever before. Lay them at his feet. Make them your heart's prayer.

⌐⫯⌐

When God does big things in the world, it is because his followers have prayed for big things to happen. Get involved. Pray big, and God will do big—more than you can think or imagine.

I correct and punish those whom I love. So be eager to do right, and change your hearts and lives.

REVELATION 3:19 NCV

When God Gives You a Time-Out

Anyone who has worked with small children is familiar with time-outs. When a child refuses to obey, smacks another tot, or infringes on other rules, he or she may be escorted to a chair for the time-out—often one minute per age. This gentle discipline system is designed to make kids stop, think about what they're doing, and make better choices. After the time-out is over, the child is free to rejoin the excitement.

As children grow up, their parents stop disciplining them, but even grownups sometimes still feel God's hand of correction. Different people respond in various manners when they face God's discipline. Some argue and refuse to admit they did anything wrong, or they put the blame on someone else. Others not only agree with God that they've done something wrong, but they also use the opportunity to beat themselves up emotionally—to go into a depression and think of how horrible they are. They hang on to the fact that they've done something wrong, and feel like a failure.

> As children grow up, their parents stop disciplining them, but even grownups sometimes still feel God's hand of correction.

Like a time-out, God's discipline isn't meant to last forever. He doesn't "spiritually spank" people to be cruel or to flaunt his power. Instead, his discipline is designed to catch a person's attention, to show her where she's wrong, and to help her think of the better choices she'll make the next time. Discipline is a sign of God's love—if he didn't love you, he wouldn't care how you act.

The next time you feel God's discipline, accept it, ask him to forgive you, and move on. God wants your heart to walk in freedom from guilt.

Here I am! I stand at the door and knock. If you hear my voice and open the door, I will come in and eat with you, and you will eat with me.

REVELATION 3:20 NCV

Real Intimacy

You know the old Uncle Sam slogan from wartime: "I want you." God has a similar slogan: "I want intimacy with you."

Jesus spoke through John to the church at Laodicea. It was a rich church, endowed with all kinds of wonderful things—buildings, treasure, a big group of people. But Jesus said they were poor because they were lukewarm. They weren't hot, and they weren't cold. Jesus used such terms to identify a person's commitment to him. A *hot* person was all out, doing all she could for God. A *cold* person had no relationship with God, and shunned him. The *lukewarm* person stood in the middle, not really committed, not all out, not willing to try anything for God, but just trying to survive from day to day.

For such lukewarm people, Jesus gave an invitation: open the door, and let's talk and eat, have fellowship, intimacy, and all the good things that come with a real relationship. God has expressed a desire to know you through and through and to have you know him. His desire is to ignite a real passion for good in you. His desire is for you to throw open the door, invite him in, and say, "Yes, let's have the kind of relationship you want with everyone." God's desire is for you to be a hot person for him.

> God has expressed a desire to know you through and through and to have you know him.

~

God stands at the door, but you have to open the door. He is there, waiting, ready, and eager. You matter to him, and he wants you to enjoy him as well as know about him.

Draw near to God and He will draw near to you. Cleanse your hands, you sinners; and purify your hearts, you double-minded.

JAMES 4:8 NKJV

"Come Over, Darlin'"

When Grace and Bruce were young, they loved to be together. They especially liked riding in Bruce's car. If Grace was sitting near the door, soon Bruce would take a corner sharply, which threw Grace toward him. "That's a COD corner, honey," he'd always say. "Come over, darlin'." Grace would always respond with a giggle and slip next to Bruce, where he could put his arm around her and they could snuggle as they rode along.

The years passed, and the two got married and started a family. During those early years, Grace would still slip in next to Bruce when he drove. They still bought cars with bench seats, but somewhere along the way, Grace stopped sliding over. The kids were in high school when one day Grace and Bruce were in the car together. She looked at Bruce and said, "We always used to snuggle so close in the car, even after the kids came along. But now you're way over there, and I'm way over here." She sighed. "What happened to us?"

> "Well, I'm where I've always been. I guess you're the one who's moved."

Bruce looked at Grace and smiled. He said, "Well, I'm where I've always been. I guess you're the one who's moved." With that, Grace grinned and slid back over.

The story about Bruce and Grace is fun, but it illustrates a serious principle. Do you ever feel distant from God? If you want to draw closer to him, just scoot closer.

God never moves away from you. He's where he's always been—just waiting to be beside you. Move a little nearer to him today.

Whatever you do, do it heartily, as to the Lord and not to men, knowing that from the Lord you will receive the reward of the inheritance; for you serve the Lord Christ.

COLOSSIANS 3:23–24 NKJV

Who Is Your Boss?

AIDS barely had a name before Dr. Daniel began working with patients stricken by the dread disease. Over the years as a university hospital doctor and a specialist in infectious diseases, he has spent many hours by the bedsides of people dying of diseases like AIDS. At times Dr. Dan's patients have told him stories of bad situations they've faced and of the rejection they've received from people who they thought loved them. Dr. Dan listens, prescribes medicine, and encourages their souls.

It isn't only the AIDS patients who appreciate Dr. Dan's care. From the sick people he encounters and the students he teaches to the foreign interns working in his office and friends, everyone feels a physical or spiritual healing touch when Dr. Dan is around. Not surprisingly, Dr. Dan is starting to become a nationally known specialist for his work. Ask Dr. Dan why he works so hard and invests himself in other people's lives so freely, and he'll tell you, "It's the job God has for me. It's the way he uses me. Since God is my boss, I do my best."

> "It's the job God has for me. It's the way he uses me. Since God is my boss, I do my best."

Maybe your job isn't that of physician, saving lives and helping ailing people. Maybe you work with a room full of rowdy elementary students. If you consider God as your real boss, you can make a difference where you are. Maybe you work all day filing records. If God is your boss and you're filing records the best you can, you will get your reward.

If you do your best and realize that you work for God, you'll find joy and satisfaction in your job, and God will reward you.

$\mathbf{W}$hatever things are true, whatever things are noble, whatever things are just, whatever things are pure, whatever things are lovely, whatever things are of good report, if there is any virtue and if there is anything praiseworthy—meditate on these things.

PHILIPPIANS 4:8 NKJV

God-Given Senior Moments

Sally jokes about having senior moments. At times she just doesn't remember things. Usually she forgets little things, and when she least expects it, the thing she's trying to remember comes to mind.

You don't have to be a senior to have senior moments. They strike women of all ages. You'll especially face them if you're busier than you'd like to be or if you're facing some stress. Senior moments are normal, and eventually your memory will clear.

It is staggering to contemplate how effectively the human memory works most of the time. Do you think your computer memory holds a lot of information? Your mind holds so much more. It is a blessing to have a healthy mind that remembers things—most of the time. The time it isn't so great is when your mind dredges up memories that are not good—such as times from the past when people hurt you or when you were embarrassed. You might also be frustrated when your mind seems to dwell on negative thoughts: discouraging news reports, problems in society, and the ugly things of life.

> You can choose to think about the good things, things that are true and godly and right.

Philippians 4:8 is a reminder that you have a choice. Your mind may flash various thoughts across its screen, but you needn't let unwelcome thoughts stay there. You needn't dwell on the negative things in life—the ugliness, the hurt, the embarrassment. You can choose to think about the good things, things that are true and godly and right.

~///○

When ugly memories or thoughts surface, ask God to give you some senior moments to forget the negative. And ask him to help you focus on the great things in your life and around you.

My God shall supply all your need according to His riches in glory by Christ Jesus.

PHILIPPIANS 4:19 NKJV

All Your Needs

Every woman has her dream. Cheryl's dream was to quit her job and stay home with her young children. She talked with her husband and prayed about it. Through her prayers, Cheryl felt God was approving her desire, so she took the plunge. She figured ways to save enough money to make up for the salary she'd brought in. Frequently she asked God to financially take care of her family. She learned they could survive without her full-time income.

God didn't mysteriously shower Cheryl's family with money. They learned to do without some things. Cheryl feels that God helped her catch tremendous sales. God provided everything Cheryl's family needed. She was even able to start an organization and Web site called Homebodies to help other moms, and she wrote two books to help women achieve their dreams to stay at home.

Philippians 4:19 gives women a wonderful reminder that God will take care of them. Usually this verse is mentioned in a fiscal context as people, like Cheryl, learn that God takes care of them financially. But the verse goes beyond that. It is a reminder that God meets every need in your life. Perhaps you have an emotional need; perhaps you

> God didn't mysteriously shower Cheryl's family with money. They learned to do without some things.

need more patience with those around you. God can meet your needs. Maybe you need encouragement and hope. God can provide it. You might even need a new washing machine. Talk to God about it. God may not provide all of your wants, but he'll meet every necessity.

It is human nature to want to be independent and take care of yourself. But give God a chance. Ask him to meet your needs and look for the obvious and subtle ways he provides.

W̲e all have different gifts, each of which came because of the grace God gave us. The person who has the gift of prophecy should use that gift in agreement with the faith.

ROMANS 12:6 NCV

You Are Gifted

Kathy loves to proofread articles and books. Most people think that proofreading—finding every little punctuation mistake and making sure everything is perfect before a page is printed—is a tedious job. But if Kathy had her way, she'd just sit in a room alone all day checking pages. She gets annoyed when she has to attend meetings or supervise other employees in her publisher's proof room.

Jennifer is Kathy's friend at the office. Jennifer loves to work on writing the books and articles that Kathy proof-reads. As it happens, Jennifer's least favorite job is proof-reading. Their boss, Bonnie, has a skill to manage people and projects. Their coworker Bruce loves to strategize to sell the products. Lynda has no desire to do any of these tasks. But she is ful-filled in doing the secretarial work that keeps the office moving. This office tends to operate smoothly—because people are in positions that they enjoy; they are in jobs that make special use of their skills.

> Every person has specific abilities God has given him or her. And each ability is important.

Every person has specific abilities God has given him or her. And each ability is important. Your skill is different from everyone else's in your office or church or family. Your skill is as vital as everyone else's. God has a place where your talent is needed. You'll find the most joy in life as you discover which gifts God has given you.

~◊

Assess your abilities. List the things you like to do most. Pursue those things wholeheartedly, knowing that God gave you gifts and skills to enjoy.

Do not let your adornment be merely outward—arranging the hair, wearing gold, or putting on fine apparel—rather let it be the hidden person of the heart, with the incorruptible beauty of a gentle and quiet spirit, which is very precious in the sight of God.

1 PETER 3:3–4 NKJV

The Imperishable Beauty Secret

Every year, millions of American women tune in to see who wins the Grammys, the Emmys, and the Oscars. Aside from talent, much of the hoopla around these events centers on what the celebrities are wearing. Some celebrities parade in outfits designed to shock; others flaunt elegant creations by world-famous designers. Jewels sparkle on arms, ears, and bodices; hair and makeup are styled to perfection.

It's tough for the average woman to look in the mirror after watching the fashion parade. Many feel the reflection looking back falls short of celebrity beauty. As a result, women spend billions of dollars choosing from millions of products that promise to make them look, smell, and feel more beautiful. At those times, God gives women the comforting reminder that outer attractiveness only

> In a world that screams for attention, a woman with a gentle and quiet spirit impresses God.

goes so far. The way you look is important, of course, but the verses in 1 Peter 3 make it clear that God prefers a greater kind of splendor—an inner splendor that is imperishable.

What God most wants to see in you is gentleness—sometimes called "power under control." This means a woman can control herself, her words, and her actions. She is powerful, respectable, and strong, and at the same time she is sweet and gentle. She is also quiet and still before God. She listens for his voice and seeks his blessing. In a world that screams for attention, a woman with a gentle and quiet spirit impresses God. She has imperishable beauty, and God calls her precious.

When it comes to trying to make yourself more beautiful, strive to develop a gentle and quiet spirit. These character traits are God's desire for you.

How precious it is, Lord, to realize that you are thinking about me constantly! I can't even count how many times a day your thoughts turn toward me. And when I waken in the morning, you are still thinking of me!

PSALM 139:17–18 TLB

Thinking of You

Being in love is such a delicious feeling. You think so much about the person you love that it is easy to become distracted. In fact, if you had a nickel for every time you thought of your beloved, you'd quickly have enough to pay for the honeymoon. You are also observant when you're in love. You notice the way he smiles, the sound of his voice, the charm of his mannerisms. Later, your mind replays every word of your conversation. People in love sometimes seem to live in a world all their own.

What a glorious feeling to discover that the one you adore has also chosen you. Knowing he loves you gives you joy, strength, and courage enough to tackle a mountain. A woman in love can be invincible.

> Knowing he loves you gives you joy, strength, and courage enough to tackle a mountain. A woman in love can be invincible.

No matter how much time you've spent thinking about a sweetheart, it is nothing compared to how much time God spends thinking about you. God watches what you do, listens to what you say, and notices everything about you. When you go to bed at night, he is thinking about you, and when you wake up in the morning, you are still on his mind.

God spends time and energy focusing on you because he loves you. When you've had a great day, God celebrates with you. When you feel alone, God is there. God loves you so much that he can't keep his mind off you.

No matter where you go or what you do, God is thinking about how terrific you are and how much he loves you.

The fear of the LORD is the beginning of wisdom, and the knowledge of the Holy One is understanding.

PROVERBS 9:10 NKJV

Finding God's Treasure

A woman learned her late husband had left treasure in their home, but she didn't know what it was. He had been a good man, cautious, kind, loving, and decent in every respect. He had never been too concerned with money or being popular. People often came to him for his counsel. His wife wondered what on earth he could have left as the treasure.

She searched all over the house but found nothing. Then one day she found a folded slip of paper in one of his dresser drawers. She remembered that her husband often took it out in the morning, read it, and voiced a quick prayer. She immediately knew this must be the treasure. She unfolded the paper and read: "This is treasure. Fear God, and everything else is easy."

> "This is treasure. Fear God, and everything else is easy."

The Bible contains many treasures, including Proverbs 9:10, the essence of the words the husband left behind. Every woman needs wisdom about how to be a godly woman, how to solve her problems, how to prosper and care for her loved ones. You can find this wisdom by first respecting and following God. You can't get all the common sense, godliness, and wisdom you need by reading books. You can't get it by watching PBS. Wisdom comes through relationship, through knowing God.

God is wise and the source of all wisdom. You can find his wisdom in the Bible. Read the Bible, memorize it, apply it, and you also will be wise.

Samuel replied, "What is more pleasing to the LORD: your burnt offerings and sacrifices or your obedience to his voice? Obedience is far better than sacrifice. Listening to him is much better than offering the fat of rams."

1 SAMUEL 15:22 NLT

Obedience vs. Sacrifice

Imagine that your boss enters your coworker's cubicle and asks her to drop everything and prepare a report for a 3:00 p.m. meeting. She says "sure" and gets busy. She looks for some data and finally finds it in a stack of papers to be filed, and so she files the stack while she's at it. As she does so, she finds two other half-finished reports and decides to quickly finish them. Then printer problems require twenty minutes. Your coworker returns to the 3:00 p.m. report. You take pity on her and help. But it isn't enough. At 3:00 p.m., your boss shows up and the report isn't quite done. "But I worked hard all day," your coworker moans. You know it's true. You feel for your coworker, but you understand your boss's perspective: though your coworker did some good things, she didn't follow the boss's orders.

> Sometimes it's easier for women to sacrifice time, resources, and energy for God instead of just doing what he told them to do.

Saul had the same kind of problem. He was sacrificing to God, and that appears to be a good thing to do. It's good, that is, unless God has told you to do something else. Saul didn't want to follow God's directives, so maybe he thought God would excuse him if he did other good things instead. But it didn't work that way. God wanted obedience.

Sometimes it's easier for women to sacrifice time, resources, and energy for God instead of just doing what he told them to do. No matter how great your sacrifices, God would rather have obedience.

～∭◯

As you obey God, the work of his kingdom will get done more efficiently and effectively. Sacrifices for God are good—but obeying his Word and directions is more important.

Speak up for those who cannot speak for themselves; defend the rights of all those who have nothing.

PROVERBS 31:8 NCV

Not Such a Personal Faith

"Religion is great, but it has no business in society." Nice sentiment, and often a popular one in society, but is it true?

Robert Raikes didn't think so. In the early 1800s in England, he became concerned about children running in the street while their parents were at work. So he used his faith to make a difference in their lives—by starting what we know today as Sunday school.

Evangeline Booth didn't think so. Her whole family left the official church structure to reach out to the needy in

England. When their ministry, called the Salvation Army, spread to the United States, Booth oversaw it. She personally helped, in Jesus's name, with unwed mothers, soup kitchens, and the forlorn of society.

A young man named Phineas Bresee worked in a Pasadena church. But Bresee felt God's call to work with the outcasts of society. He was kicked out of his church for this interest in "bad characters"—and he became the father of a denomination, the Church of the Nazarene, that focused both on honoring Jesus and on making a social difference.

> People who love God go ahead. They speak out for the poor, the needy, the unborn, and others who can't speak out for themselves.

These are just a few stories of people who've changed society by refusing to let someone make them keep their faith off the streets. People who love God go ahead. They speak out for the poor, the needy, the unborn, and others who can't speak out for themselves.

—∭

If you feel called to serve God or to be a witness in a social arena, go for it. Let your faith change your life and change your world.

People may make plans in their minds, but the Lord decides what they will do.

Proverbs 16:9 ncv

God's To-Do List

The modern to-do list became a household practice in the early 1900s. A wise consultant had shown one of the captains of industry this simple method of organizing his day. It is said that the capitalist paid this consultant thousands of dollars for the idea. Today many women use this method of organizing their lives. They put it on a PDA, type it into the computer, print it neatly in a notebook, or scrawl it on a slip of paper. Sometimes there are various to-do lists for different areas of responsibility. These lists allow you to plot out your time for maximum effectiveness.

You, however, should consider still another to-do list — God's to-do list. Proverbs 16:9 reveals that God has actually planned your day, too, filling it with good things for you to accomplish for him and his kingdom. You may not know what is

> Take a look at how you plan your day, and ask God what you should add to your to-do list.

coming. You may not be thinking about his plans for you. But they're there. You should include him in your plans because he ultimately controls what happens in life everywhere.

Take a look at how you plan your day, and ask God what you should add to your to-do list. Maybe he'll put into your mind that task you've been avoiding or the name of someone you should visit. Perhaps he'll encourage you to prepare that incredible dinner you've been telling the family about.

Trust God to give you the insight you need in your plans. Ask him to participate. Give him priority. What he most desires is that you be fulfilled.

Let him who thinks he stands take heed lest he fall.

1 CORINTHIANS 10:12 NKJV

No Shaky Ground

An older woman created a stir in her church when she went to the pastor's wife to offer some advice about how to conduct her ministry. The old woman had filled a legal sheet of paper with criticisms and remedies for the pastor's wife. Needless to say, the pastor's wife was overwhelmed and hurt, and she felt like a failure. She couldn't bear to be around the older woman and didn't talk to her for days.

Something happened one day, though, when the older woman's son visited his mother. He voiced several concerns about attitudes he saw in his mother's life. One of the attitudes he pointed out happened to be the very thing the older woman had accused the pastor's wife of doing. Her son's words struck home, and the older woman's tender heart was touched. She realized how she must have hurt the pastor's wife.

> **Evaluate your life and make sure you're not taking credit for something God has done in you.**

She went to that pastor's wife to encourage her. Soon they became close friends, relying on each other for counsel, wisdom, and encouragement.

People tend to criticize others about the same issues they need to work on. When you're feeling proud or sure that you're such a good person, remember 1 Corinthians 10:12 and put on a bit of humility, a bit of there-but-for-the-grace-of-God-go-I. Evaluate your life and make sure you're not taking credit for something God has done in you.

When you focus your eye on your neighbor, you are likely to make a big mistake that you'll regret for weeks to come. Strive for humility and acceptance of others. God will bless that outlook.

The only temptation that has come to you
is that which everyone has. But you can
trust God, who will not permit you to be
tempted more than you can stand. But
when you are tempted, he will also give
you a way to escape so that you will be
able to stand it.

1 CORINTHIANS 10:13 NCV

The Escape Hatch

In the fourth century, asceticism rose to its highest popularity. Ascetics were people who typically denied themselves the usual comforts of sleep, food, water, bed, and home. They did this, they believed, to avoid temptation. For instance, Saint Ascepsimas wore numerous chains to remind himself of his penchant for temptation. Brother Besarion, a monk, refused sleep, and wouldn't lie down for forty years. Saint Maron lived in a hollow tree trunk, where he was supposedly safe from the influences of the world. There have been stories of ascetics in modern times who self-deny in the belief that to do so will obtain for them a higher spiritual or moral state.

Such measures do little to stop temptation. Instead, the Bible provides a far superior remedy. If one verse in the Bible stands out as a guide for dealing with temptation, 1 Corinthians 10:13 is it. Everyone faces temptation. You can't escape it. When you admit temptation is there and get prayer help, you find that others have faced the same thing. You can claim God's promise that he won't let temptation become so strong that you have to give in. He

> You can claim God's promise that he won't let temptation become so strong that you have to give in.

will guide you to an incredible escape hatch. Running and fleeing the temptation, resisting the temptation, or finding something else to do are all good strategies.

You don't have to give in to temptation, but God encourages you to turn to him for help, guidance, and comfort.

The next time temptation taunts you, turn to God and ask him to show you his way of escape. He will, and you'll be free.

Be kind and loving to each other, and forgive each other just as God forgave you in Christ.

EPHESIANS 4:32 NCV

"I Remember Forgetting That"

Clara Barton founded the Red Cross, a corps of nurses and doctors who treated the wounded during the Civil War. Clara had a great heart for kindness and compassion toward all people. A fellow nurse once mentioned a wrong that a mutual friend had done to Clara. Asked if she remembered the incident, Clara replied, "I distinctly remember forgetting that one."

Kindness and compassion are qualities every woman should develop. Those qualities help you enjoy friendly and cordial relationships. Many stories have been told about how kindness won the day when strength, hardness, and determined resistance only led to war. At times, strength is necessary. More often, kindness and compassion change both the giver and the receiver. Ephesians 4:32 tells you to offer friendship, understanding,

> At times, strength is necessary. More often, kindness and compassion change both the giver and the receiver.

and forgiveness, not only to your friends, but also to those who sin against you. The same way Jesus erased your sins and promises never to bring them up again, so he expects you to offer forgiveness to those who hurt you.

Clara Barton revealed a second level of forgiveness that you shouldn't miss. Her remembering to "forget that one" is how you should forgive. Sometimes it takes a while to get a hurt out of your mind. The way to deal with it is to refuse to dwell on it and simply decide not to dredge up all the details. Just put it out of your mind every time it occurs to you.

~

Forgiveness is a process. The day after someone wrongs you may make your forgiveness tough, but if you won't let the wrong simmer and stir within you, eventually it will be gone forever.

Keep your lives free from the love of money, and be satisfied with what you have. God has said, "I will never leave you; I will never forget you."

HEBREWS 13:5 NCV

Never Alone

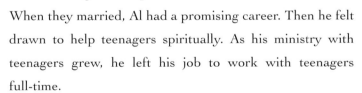

Al and Vidy never had much money. They were both raised during the depression. When they married, Al had a promising career. Then he felt drawn to help teenagers spiritually. As his ministry with teenagers grew, he left his job to work with teenagers full-time.

Over the years, Al and Vidy poured most of their small salary back into their ministry to teens. They fixed up a little house to use as rental property to help put their three kids through school. Along the way, they gave up some financial dreams. Vidy had always wanted a fur coat, but decided her wool one would do fine. Al had always wanted a nice car, but the closest he ever got was a fifteen-year-old Cadillac that someone gave them.

Al and Vidy didn't really feel the sacrifices. They were happy that they could make a difference in teen lives. They had learned the secret of great living: their love for each other and their relationship with God were more important than any money or possessions could be. They have rejoiced to see their children and grandchildren follow in their footsteps. Some of them even run the youth organization that Al and Vidy started sixty years ago. Al is gone now, but Vidy doesn't feel alone. She knows that God is with her and that he has provided every need. She is satisfied.

> Once in a while every woman should take a measure of her life and assess what is really important.

Once in a while every woman should take a measure of her life and assess what is really important. Vidy's attitude is an example that all women can follow.

The advertising world puts pressure on people to accumulate things and money. But the greatest accomplishments you can have are contentment and contented relationships with God and other people.

Be imitators of God as dear children.

EPHESIANS 5:1 NKJV

A Chip off the Old Block

In 1963, an executive from the Kenner toy company realized that the toy industry was turning out a lot of new, exciting toys for boys but that it wasn't doing much for girls. So he came up with the idea of producing an inexpensive oven for girls that looked just like Mom's. And the Easy-Bake Oven was born. Over the years, as oven styles changed, so did the Easy-Bake Oven so that girls could continue to emulate their mothers. After a few years, there were even little Betty Crocker mixes that looked like the ones the adults used but were created especially for the little ovens.

Kenner didn't originate the idea of creating toys that are mini-versions of tools adults use. Many museums around the country display toy farm equipment, toy kitchen equipment, and other minia-ture versions of adult paraphernalia.

> **From the begin-ning of time, kids have emulated their parents and other grownups.**

From the beginning of time, kids have emulated their parents and other grownups.

One of the joys of being around preschoolers and early elementary–age children is watching them observe and mimic teachers' and parents' words, behaviors, and attitudes. It's intriguing to see children grow up to be just like their fathers or mothers.

This is the illustration Paul gives in Ephesians 5:1. Since you are a child of God, Paul encourages you to imitate God — to act the way God would, to speak the kind of words God would speak, to think like and to become like God in every way.

Ask God to help his Spirit become so ingrained in you that those who meet you instantly see glimpses of your Father.

Among you there must not be even a hint of sexual immorality, or of any kind of impurity, or of greed, because these are improper for God's holy people.

EPHESIANS 5:3 NIV

The Power of Purity

You needed to be around Georgia for only a few hours to realize that you'd never hear a raucous or off-color joke come out of her mouth. It wasn't that she didn't have a great sense of humor—she did. And it wasn't that she was a prude about sex—she and her husband were honest about their deep love for each other and about the physical pleasures they still enjoyed as they entered their senior years. It wasn't even that Georgia was outdated—she'd spent her whole life working with teenagers and was still "hip." She wasn't naive; she was simply pure. Georgia had learned early in life that the Bible tells women to be reflections of God in all they say and do, and she quickly learned the importance of *garbage in garbage out*—that what a person puts into her life will show up in her actions, attitudes, and words.

Georgia put good things into her mind and life, and it shows. As a result, she has earned the respect of all kinds of people. She has been able to make a difference in individual lives, and even in communities. When Georgia speaks, people listen because they know Georgia's words will be well thought out, honest, and honorable.

> There's power in a pure heart, a stainless mind, and a clean tongue.

There's power in a pure heart, a stainless mind, and a clean tongue. A woman doesn't have to live in a Pollyanna world, but she can discipline what goes into her heart and mind. As she puts God-honoring things into her life, purity will shine out.

Ask God to show you ways you can reflect his holiness and cleanness in your world. Strive to be clean in your actions, your thoughts, and your words.

When you talk, do not say harmful things, but say what people need—words that will help others become stronger. Then what you say will do good to those who listen to you.

EPHESIANS 4:29 NCV

Putting Teeth to Your Words

One strange facet of nature is the snail's tongue. Long like a ribbon and kept rolled up until it's needed, the snail's tongue contains more than thirty thousand teeth embedded in it. With those teeth, the snail can saw through and consume leaves, stems, and other edible, leafy parts.

Like the snail, some human tongues also contain teeth, figuratively speaking. However, that's not necessarily negative. Just as the snail uses its powerful teeth for good—sawing through leaves and getting nourishment—so can you put powerful teeth behind your tongue and help others. Don't complain or criticize, but put teeth into your words by encouraging, giving, and nurturing. Speak words of light, life, and love.

Ephesians 4:29 tells you how to use your tongue if you want to please God. Say things that are good and speak to the need of the moment. Do you see someone who is hurting and broken? Speak words of hope. Have you crossed paths with a friend today who is troubled and worried? Reach into your heart and find words that will saw into that pain and cut it out of the soul. When you use your tongue to speak such words, you will find that people draw close to you and will listen gladly to your wisdom, stories, thoughts, and concerns.

> Don't complain or criticize, but put teeth into your words by encouraging, giving, and nurturing.

~

An old proverb says to "think before you speak." Before you speak, think about the need of the moment and of how others might be built up. Put teeth into your words.

Our fight is not against people on earth
but against the rulers and authorities and
the powers of this world's darkness,
against the spiritual powers of evil in
the heavenly world.

EPHESIANS 6:12 NCV

The Right Battlefield

Sometimes Fran becomes dismayed. As she reads the daily newspapers, she often feels heaviness in her heart. She wants to do something to counter people who promote illicit sex or try to curb religious expression. She doesn't like confrontations with outsiders.

Ephesians 6:12 tells another story of the world. It isn't you versus "them." Instead, it's you plus God, God's people, and God's angels versus the real enemies of God—demons, fallen angels, and Satan. You are not alone. It isn't your battle. It is a battle the whole world is engaged in, and God is on your side. Seeing the world through the lens of Ephesians 6:12 will change your perspective. God is in this with you. It isn't the people of the world you must fight, but forces beyond this world who simply use those people as their pawns.

When you feel evil in the world, you are not fighting against other people. The people who think it is okay to take a life or act in an immoral manner aren't your enemies. Instead, the battle rages on a spiritual level all about you. That's where the true battle rages. From that spiritual plane come the temptations, deceptions, and scams that fill your world. When you do battle in prayer or service, or when you tell others the good news that God loves them, you are battling those forces as much as anything in this world.

> **It isn't the people of the world you must fight, but forces beyond this world who simply use those people as their pawns.**

~

The true battle is on a spiritual plane. You must fight it with God's spiritual tools—truthfulness, righteousness, peacemaking. Use those tools, and victory will be God's and yours.

Great is our Lord, and mighty in power;
His understanding is infinite.

PSALM 147:5 NKJV

He Understands

Friends, moms, and God all tend to have something in common: they understand. Think of a person in your life who is a good friend. You have probably spent hours together and shared many experiences. As a result, you understand each other. The more you communicate, the more you understand each other's perspective and understand where the other person is coming from. You may not always agree with your friend's choices, but you probably understand why she made them.

The same may be true if you have children or are around them. If you watch children to figure out what makes them tick, what motivates them, you'll better understand the reasons why they do some of the things they do. For instance, when you realize your child is afraid of monsters under the bed, you have a little more patience and understanding when he or she doesn't want to sleep in his room alone.

> **God knows everything about you, good and bad, and loves you thoroughly.**

One of the most glorious facts about having a relationship with God is the realization that he understands your deepest desires and hopes. He realizes the temptations you face. He knows how hard you try. God knows everything about you, good and bad, and loves you thoroughly. Because he understands you so well, you can trust him and turn to him at any time.

Never hesitate to turn to God in your joy, or in your challenges. He understands your motivations, your struggles, and your faith.

Among you there must
not be even a hint of sexual
immorality, or of any kind
of impurity, or of greed,
because these are improper
for God's holy people.

EPHESIANS 5:3 NIV

Rejoice in the Lord always. Again I will say, rejoice!

PHILIPPIANS 4:4 NKJV

True Joy

Andi stared out the office window at the bluebirds nesting in her little birdhouse. Smiling, she said "Thank you, Lord" under her breath. A few moments later, as she filed some papers, she found herself singing a song she'd heard on the radio. Belting out the words filled her with a joy she couldn't explain. She suddenly found herself bowing at her desk and praying, "Lord, you are so good. Thank you for all the blessings of today and every day. I feel like shouting 'Hallelujah' wherever I go."

Andi had learned a new habit over the last few months: rejoicing in the Lord. The idea came from Philippians 4:4, surely one of the great truths for a time in history when so many people are attacking, hurting, complaining, and criticizing. When you think about it, there are many things to rejoice in about God, with God, and for God. Think about your senses. Taste, touch, hearing, seeing, smelling. What miracles they are.

> As you become more used to rejoicing, thanking, and praising, you will feel freer about it and more natural.

They are great things to rejoice in. Your home, your country, your job. God enjoys it when you rejoice in these gifts.

Rejoicing in the Lord is something God wants you to cultivate in your life. It takes a little effort at first, some thinking and some reflecting. As you become more used to rejoicing, thanking, and praising, you will feel freer about it and more natural.

Nothing is more natural than being glad for someone's presence, care, love, or gifts. Let God know when you appreciate the things he has put into your life. It will refresh him and you.

You see that Abraham's faith and the things he did worked together. His faith was made perfect by what he did.

JAMES 2:22 NCV

Doing or Believing?

Many people have struggled with the meaning of James 2:22. Is believing the right things most important? Or is doing the right things most important? Clearly, behavior is important. What you do to someone else can hurt that person, while your beliefs may simply be a point of disagreement. God wants all people to treat one another rightly, to do good with their lives, and to serve each other in real terms, like helping an elderly neighbor get to the doctor, babysitting for a harried mother, or giving a cheering word to a coworker.

On the other hand, faith is also important. Trusting God—building a relationship with him and becoming intimate friends—is of great importance. How do doing good and believing in God relate? Some people believe doing good is what life is all about, while others say faith is paramount.

The verse from James highlights the powerful truth that faith and doing good go together. Faith produces a heart and life that seek to do what is right and helpful. Faith comes first, but quickly following are the good character, deeds, thoughts, and words of a person who loves God. You can't have one without

> **Your life changes when you truly believe. God works in your heart to produce a humble, godly, life-honoring, and life-building person.**

the other. Your life changes when you truly believe. God works in your heart to produce a humble, godly, life-honoring, and life-building person.

Faith becomes perfect or mature when you let your faith tell your mouth, heart, and body to do good for everyone. When this attitude characterizes your lifestyle, you will truly be a "woman of faith" in God's eyes.

He has taken our sins away from us as far as the east is from the west.

PSALM 103:12 NCV

No Fishing

If you're like the rest of humanity, at some time or another, you've probably done something wrong. One of the worst things about committing a sin is that humans have memories. Long after a woman has asked God and others to forgive her for what she has done wrong, the memories linger. Her memory plays them over and over again, pounding out her joy and confidence. While God does want a person to ask for forgiveness when she has sinned and to decide to do right, he never intended for anyone who loves him to carry the shame and guilt of sins forever. In fact, Psalm 103:12 says that when a person has asked God to forgive her for her wrongdoings, he doesn't leave those sins heaped in a pile around her. Instead, he takes those sins out of her

> **God has no interest in dredging up your sins that he has already forgiven.**

presence; he takes them from her as far as he can—as far as east is from west, which basically means eternally.

Corrie ten Boom, a Holocaust concentration camp survivor, used to say that when a person has asked forgiveness for sins, God throws those sins into the deepest sea, where they are irretrievable. Then, according to Corrie, he puts up a sign that reads "No Fishing."

God has no interest in dredging up your sins that he has already forgiven. He has no interest in making you pay for your sins over and over. After all, that's the reason why Jesus Christ lived and was crucified—so you can be released from every wrong word, thought, and action you've ever hosted.

⌐⫯⊙

If memories of past sins and errors are dogging you, make your own little "No Fishing" sign to remind you of what God has done. And enjoy living in freedom from guilt.

Walk in the Spirit, and you shall not fulfill the lust of the flesh.

GALATIANS 5:16 NKJV

A Walk with a Friend

You're taking a long walk with a close friend. What happens on this little adventure? You talk some; your friend responds. The friend brings up a subject; you both discuss it. Your walk together involves talking, thinking, reacting, posing questions, offering answers, and simply enjoying each other's presence. You might say hello to people passing by, and comment on what's going on down a certain street. A walk with a friend isn't simply a means to get somewhere; it is also the process of getting there that's important and part of the fun of it.

The Bible often compares the biblical lifestyle to a walk. As you go through life, you recognize that God's Spirit is there with you, counseling, consoling, offering advice, giving encouragement, pointing out wrong thoughts or attitudes. God's Spirit, like a best friend on a walk, desires that you enjoy his presence and learn to embrace him all day, every day.

> God's Spirit, like a best friend on a walk, desires that you enjoy his presence and learn to embrace him all day, every day.

This verse from Galatians teaches you the vital truth that if you follow the Holy Spirit, he will help you do what's right always and never to do what is wrong. As the Bible teaches, it's like a walk or a stroll where God's Spirit becomes a real and vibrant part of your life. With him there, you will naturally turn away from wrong and do good.

Walking by the Spirit is not difficult. Ask him to reveal himself to you. Then proceed, expecting him to speak, guide, encourage, and point out any wrong path you might be taking.

I have been young, and now am old; yet I have not seen the righteous forsaken, nor his descendants begging bread.

PSALM 37:25 NKJV

Never Forsaken

An Indian woman at a missions conference in Calcutta stood before a large crowd and held up hands with only a few fingers. Because her body was ravaged by leprosy, it was hard for many even to look at her. But her face was radiant. "Thank God," she said. "Thank God for my leprosy. For because of it, I came to know him. I was drawn to him because of my suffering, and I became a believer in him when I realized his love and goodness. From that time, I have never been hungry or thirsty, and I have helped many others find in him the answer to their deepest needs." She then quoted Psalm 37:25, adding that it had proved true in her life.

God sometimes guides circumstances, whether good or bad, in order to draw you closer to himself. At times you may have a need because he wants you to turn to him for help. When he answers, he will be glorified and your faith will be built up. This verse from the Psalms shows you the powerful truth that God never leaves his children begging. He will always respond to your needs and meet them on his timetable. You can trust that he has allowed that need to exist because he wants you to pray and ask him to meet it.

> God sometimes guides circumstances, whether good or bad, in order to draw you closer to himself.

This verse is central for you because it reminds you that when you're living for God, he is going to see that you are taken care of. He will care for you emotionally and materially, and will care for you and your children.

─᠊᠊᠊᠊᠊

Take a hard look at your life. You probably have new needs every day. Turn to God and watch him supply, and then you can tell the world how God really does supply everything.

To the woman [the LORD God] said: "I will greatly multiply your sorrow and your conception; in pain you shall bring forth children; your desire shall be for your husband, and he shall rule over you."

GENESIS 3:16 NKJV

Pains of Joy

God cursed humankind when Adam and Eve sinned in the Garden of Eden. That curse left the human race with numerous problems, including pain in childbirth for women and man's fight to overcome weeds and thistles in trying to produce food. Even today, people feel the results of that curse. Bearing a child is monumentally painful. Many men feel unfulfilled in their work, or that they have never produced anything worthwhile in their lives.

What is the solution? There is an important answer for women in this verse about the pain Eve would feel in having children. It's just like God to give back with his right hand what his left hand has taken. In the midst of the curse, he offered a great promise: you will still have children. You will still love your husband. You will still enjoy sexual desire. Even when God levies a terrible curse, he provides a tremendous blessing beyond it.

> **Even when God levies a terrible curse, he provides a tremendous blessing beyond it.**

God promised in his statement to Eve that great blessing would come even in the midst of a curse. Every woman who has given birth by natural means knows the meaning of God's curse. But God did not leave labor without hope. After the baby is born joy results, and the curse of labor is forgotten. In the place of pain comes great jubilation.

When you are feeling the pangs of a sinful world, remember, God will give you fulfillment even though you must travel some hard paths to get to it.

My people mingle with the heathen, picking up their evil ways; thus they become as good-for-nothing as a half-baked cake!

HOSEA 7:8 TLB

Half-Baked Cakes

Although no one seems to know the exact history of pancakes, apparently even the earliest civilizations quickly learned that ground-up grain and water made a basic pancake. Over the years, people learned that ingredients like eggs and baking powder made the cakes lighter. Now you can find pancakes made out of all sorts of grain ingredients, with myriad stuffings and toppings. Patty tells about the chocolate-chip pancakes her mom used to make. "They were really thick," Patty explains. "Mom mixed the chocolate chips into the batter and poured it into the pan."

Patty loved those pancakes—usually. "Sometimes the pancake would look done. But when I cut into it, raw batter would ooze out. It was pretty disgusting."

Half-cooked pancakes not only taste bad, but they also carry a threat of salmonella poisoning from the raw eggs. And you can't take a half-cooked pancake, flip it back on the grill, and make it good—for the inside to heat more, the outside would get rubbery. You can't do anything with a half-cooked pancake except throw it away.

> You can't do anything with a half-cooked pancake except throw it away.

A half-baked cake or pancake is the illustration Hosea gave in the Scripture tackling the paramount issue of trying to live between two worlds spiritually. The person doesn't really want to live wholly like a God-follower; but on the other hand, nor does he want to live like someone who isn't a God-follower. As a result, the person doesn't fit anywhere and is about as useful as a half-raw pancake.

~

Keep serving God with a wholehearted commitment. Place your total faith in him, and every day explore ways you can serve him better.

Behold, I am the LORD, the God of all flesh. Is there anything too hard for Me?

JEREMIAH 32:27 NKJV

A Competent God

As a child, Sarah thought of her mom as Mrs. Fix-It. When a doll's arm came off one time, Sarah took it to Mom and she fixed it. When Sarah struggled to understand arithmetic in grade school, Mom spent hours drilling her, and Sarah is a math whiz today. In high school and college, Mom fixed Sarah's troubles with boys, English comp, soccer, and other matters. For Sarah, her mom continues to be a force in her life for good. She can do just about anything.

Of course, in reality there are many things Sarah's mom can't do. She can't automatically fix a difficult marriage or give her daughter more time to get things done. She can't make a baby's handicap go away. And she certainly can't solve the problem of death or serious illness. But there is Someone who can help her much as her mother did, but who is far greater and stronger: God. Sarah can lean on her heavenly Parent for strength, courage, and wisdom to deal with the hard things in her life.

> God can do anything—any-thing—as long as it does not compromise his holiness and righteousness.

At times in your life, the situation may seem hopeless and your circumstances insurmountable. The joy is torn from your life. You are not alone, however. The situation isn't forever, and nothing is too hard for God. God can do any-thing—anything—as long as it does not compromise his holi-ness and righteousness.

God is the ultimate Mr. Fix-It. He doesn't fix everything in a day or even in a lifetime. But look to him for the answers to your concerns, and eventually the answers will come.

Call to Me, and I will answer you, and show you great and mighty things, which you do not know.

JEREMIAH 33:3 NKJV

Call to Him

Everyone loves getting an invitation. "It's a party. Come one, come all." "We want you. Be there or be square." "Give me a call when you have a chance. I'd like to talk." Invitations are always welcomed. It means you're special, you're important, you're a valuable person.

An invitation from God, though? A call into his throne room? A chance to sit at his feet and just drink in the atmosphere? It's right there in Jeremiah 33. God has given you the invitation of all time. He literally commands you to go to him. Spend time together. Talk. Converse. Listen. Learn. Or just enjoy being with each other. He invites you to spend time with him alone. This verse is not for the special few. This is not written to the royals. God gets personal. He wants to make your life fulfilling and happy.

Think about it. When you call on God, you never get a busy signal or an answering machine. You never hear, "Hey, I'm doing something right now. Call again later." Or, "Look, I'm into a big problem at the moment, so bug off." God is always

> God gets personal. He wants to make your life fulfilling and happy.

available. Not only will he be there when you call, but you can know God's true heart. He will not only answer, but he will take a step further: he will tell you other things, great and hidden things, fresh insights that you haven't known. He'll give you the real scoop on anything you want to know.

Call on God today. Ask him a question, any question. Share a concern. Consider a thought. This is God's invitation to you, and it lasts forever.

He will not allow your foot to be moved;
He who keeps you will not slumber.
Behold, He who keeps Israel shall neither
slumber nor sleep.

PSALM 121:3–4 NKJV

While You Were Sleeping

Have you ever been awakened by a strange noise? You sit up in bed and listen intently. You might turn on a light and go investigate if the noise continues. Perhaps you'll pick up a baseball bat or some other weapon, just in case it's someone who's not supposed to be there. But then you share a laugh when the real culprit appears—the neighbor's cat, or the wind blowing leaves around the yard.

For the person living in ancient Israel, it was great comfort to know that God never sleeps. It is comfort today as well. God stands guard over you. You needn't fear marauders, robbers, or assailants, for God remains watchful. You and your valuables are safe all night long. You can entrust yourself to him, knowing he would never slip away for a drink or doze on his shift.

> For the person living in ancient Israel, it was great comfort to know that God never sleeps. It is comfort today as well.

In the day of alarm systems, watchdogs, and other devices for protection, you don't often fear what might happen while you're asleep. Despite the many terrors that surround those who love God, you can feel safe. As a woman, you can take comfort in the God who won't be caught off guard. God will protect you all along life's path without letting you slide on the slippery rocks of the world's greatest dangers.

If you find the nighttime a frightening time, take heart in the grand truth that God is always there, watching, protecting, making sure you arrive in heaven safely.

Open my eyes to see the miracles in your teachings.

PSALM 119:18 NCV

Fresh Truth

Beth drove down the highway, headed home for Christmas. Many hours into the drive, tired of listening to the radio, she just wished she could hurry up and get there. She didn't want to stop because she had promised to get there by Christmas morning, no later. She finally prayed and asked God what to do. She sensed him telling her to meditate on a verse of the Bible. In her mind, she thought about the Christmas story, of Joseph and Mary bringing Jesus into the world in a stable. She had memorized the whole seven verses just that month.

As she roved over the sentences, insights filled her mind. How dangerous for Mary and Joseph to travel many miles, and she was nine months pregnant, sitting on a donkey. She realized that Mary and Joseph went to Bethlehem, where prophecy said the Messiah would be born, because of Caesar's decree. And then another thought: how did anyone know it was a stable? Luke never said anything about a stable. But, aha, there it was: Mary laid Jesus in the manger. Mangers were for cows and donkeys, so it was probably a stable, but it might have been something else altogether. Excitement flooded her mind as more insights came to her. Soon she was more awake than ever.

> When Bible study gets stale, ask the Lord to give you new insights, an idea you've never thought of before, or a measure of understanding that goes beyond your years and education.

Do you find that sometimes Bible reading gets old? God will speak to you as you study the Bible. When Bible study gets stale, ask the Lord to give you new insights, an idea you've never thought of before, or a measure of understanding that goes beyond your years and education. He will do it, if you ask.

God does not want your time in the Bible to be boring or a waste of time or even meaningless. Look to him for the insights that lead to spiritual excitement. He promises to give you that blessing.

"The God who made you is like your husband. His name is the LORD All-Powerful. The Holy One of Israel is the one who saves you. He is called the God of all the earth. You were like a woman whose husband left her, and you were very sad. You were like a wife who married young and then her husband left her. But the LORD called you to be his," says your God.

ISAIAH 54:5–6 NCV

When God Steps In

One of the biggest shifts in trends during the past few decades has been the compilation of the family. Once upon a time, the average family included a husband, wife, and kids. There were deviations from that, but it was the standard. Today that's not true. According to the U.S. Census Bureau report, single households and single-parent households make up more than half of all households in the United States. Although a woman may have a husband during some period in her life, that doesn't mean she'll always have a mate. It is also true that some husbands are absent physically or emotionally, and even a great spouse can't always meet all the needs in a woman's life.

> **God promises to always be with you and to be actively involved in your life.**

If you don't have a husband to help provide the finances for your home, God can help. If you don't have a husband to be your companion, God promises to always be with you and to be actively involved in your life. If you need help making decisions, God promises to give wisdom. When you feel a longing to be needed and wanted, remember, God called you to be his. If you want someone to talk to, God will always listen. God is willing to fill any and all empty niches in your life.

If you don't have a husband, or if your husband isn't meeting your needs, don't fret, panic, or give in to discouragement. Let God step in and be your strength, provider, protection, and friend.

Better a little with righteousness than much gain with injustice.

Proverbs 16:8 NIV

Money Isn't Everything

T.J. was almost living his dream job. He was working as a human resources director for a small but growing airline. The only thing he would have liked better would be taking the pilot's seat. After September 11, 2001, T.J.'s airline suffered. The company tried to get government aid but was unsuccessful. Other companies considered buying his airline.

One prospective buyer was a restaurant chain well known for capitalizing on sexual suggestiveness. T.J. did not accept the morals of the company. But if the company bought the airline and T.J. left his job on an ethical basis, not only would he be giving up his dream job, but he knew most places would not pay him as well.

Perhaps you've faced a situation similar to T.J.'s. Perhaps you've been offered great money on a job if you'd expose half your body or if you'd turn your head when the corporation tried unethical or downright illegal business practices. Perhaps you have faced the dilemma of getting promoted if you're willing to lie for the boss or if you'd let an important client's hand wander where it shouldn't.

> **Money can be a wonderful, fun tool in the world, but although money is nice, it is better to have integrity and to live your convictions.**

If you've ever encountered situations like this, Proverbs 16:8 is for you. If you haven't yet faced this situation, this verse will help set your heart so you'll go the right direction. Money can be a wonderful, fun tool in the world, but although money is nice, it is better to have integrity and to live your convictions.

Always choose the honest, ethical, beyond-reproach way. You may not have as much money, but God will take care of your needs.

If you remain completely silent at this time, relief and deliverance will arise for the Jews from another place, but you and your father's house will perish. Yet who knows whether you have come to the kingdom for such a time as this?

ESTHER 4:14 NKJV

For Such a Time as This

Esther was a beautiful woman—inside and out. So it wasn't a surprise when she was chosen to be the queen. She seemed to enjoy this position—until one day she learned that the king's adviser planned to annihilate all the Jewish people. The thought that your husband is destroying a whole race is shocking enough. But for Esther, it had an extra traumatic twist. The king and his adviser didn't know she was Jewish.

Esther could have been concerned only about saving her own neck. But her uncle pointed out the fact that perhaps God had put her in a position of power to be his tool for rescuing his people, that God might have put her in the palace "for such a time as this."

Esther's reaction reveals that she was wise as well as beautiful. Instead of panicking, she prayed. She gathered other Jewish people to fast and pray. She engaged every bit of the femininity and brains God had given her, and God used her to save her people. She truly was in the right place at the right time for a reason.

> God has a place and a purpose for you. You are part of his divine design.

Just as he had a place and a purpose for Esther, God has a place and a purpose for you. You are part of his divine design. You may be involved in a certain school or organization, not by chance, but for some reason that only God knows about at this point. You might have formed a new acquaintance for a reason you know nothing about.

Keep serving God and looking for his guidance. He will keep you in the right place at the right time and use you to make a difference. What looks like normal circumstances to you may actually be divine appointments.

The LORD said to Samuel, "Don't look at how handsome Eliab is or how tall he is, because I have not chosen him. God does not see the same way people see. People look at the outside of a person, but the LORD looks at the heart." 1 SAMUEL 16:7 NCV

How Is Your Heart?

Marta sat with her mother and spilled out her thoughts and feelings. She tried hard to articulate all that was in her heart, and she found her mother's smiling prods and encouragement empowering. As she talked, her mother said, "I understand. Yes, I get that. I've felt that way too." When she finished, she exclaimed, "You really do understand what I'm talking about." "I've been there too, darling," was her mother's reply.

The heart—not the organ, but the center of the emotions and personality—is a delicate, mysterious element of the human psyche. It receives, records, and responds to all the data that come at it in a day. What Marta was experiencing is something all people know: no one can really know what goes on in your heart unless you tell him. But when you do, the light of understanding and identification comes on. It is a wonderful feeling to find someone who agrees with you and comprehends the feelings you may be trying to express.

> God sees the heart of each person and knows its deepest thoughts, longings, hopes, and fears.

In the same way, God sees the heart of each person and knows its deepest thoughts, longings, hopes, and fears. Cling to 1 Samuel 16:7 to realize that God knows you better than any other person. God sees not just the outward appearance, which varies greatly woman to woman, but he sees the true center of existence, the heart.

⌐⁂◦

When you feel frustrated that you can't articulate a feeling or concern, or when you wonder if anyone really knows the depth of your feelings, find hope in God. He knows you through to the heart.

You prepare a table before me in the presence of my enemies; You anoint my head with oil; my cup runs over. Surely goodness and mercy shall follow me all the days of my life; and I will dwell in the house of the LORD forever.

PSALM 23:5–6 NKJV

You Are the Guest of Honor

You are invited to a party, a surprise party. For whom? For you. Don't be too amazed. It is going to happen. The party will be thrown in your honor to show the whole world what kind of woman you really were in life. All the marvels of your great thoughts, words, and deeds will be shown for all to see and praise. Many people will be stunned to find out how much God thought of you, because some said your life didn't really amount to much. Nonetheless, God saw things no one else did, and that's why he is throwing the party.

It is going to happen, and the grand truth is expressed in Psalm 23. God will sit you down before all people from all nations, places, times, and races. He will serve you the best meal possible— filet mignon, swordfish steak, whatever you most like. He will anoint

> **God will fill your cup till it overflows.**

your head with a fine perfume, showing not only respect and love but the fact that you are royalty in his house. God will fill your cup till it overflows.

You may wonder long and hard about when this will happen, but God assures his beloved saints in these verses the wonderful truth that he will never embarrass you, put you down, or humiliate you before others when you get to heaven. Rather, he spreads his feast before you for you to enjoy. He even honors you in front of those who may not have liked or respected you. You will dwell in God's house forever.

～⁂

One day you will sit before all creation, and God himself will honor you. That is what he does for all his friends.

Open my eyes to see the
miracles in your teachings.

PSALM 119:18 NCV

God began doing a good work in you,
and I am sure he will continue it until it is
finished when Jesus Christ comes again.

PHILIPPIANS 1:6 NCV